GROWING
MARIJUANA

GROWING MARIJUANA

How to Plant, Cultivate, and Harvest Your Own Weed

Tommy McCarthy

Skyhorse Publishing

Skyhorse Publishing books may be purchased in bulk at special
discounts for sales promotion, corporate gifts, fund-raising, or
educational purposes. Special editions can also be created to specifications.
For details, contact the Special Sales Department,
Skyhorse Publishing, 307 West 36th Street, 11th Floor, New York,
NY 10018 or info@skyhorsepublishing.com.

Skyhorse® and Skyhorse Publishing® are registered trademarks
of Skyhorse Publishing, Inc. ®, a Delaware corporation.

www.skyhorsepublishing.com

15 14 13 12 11 10 9 8 7 6

Photo on page 146 by www.rudeboyimaging.com.

Library of Congress Cataloging-in-Publication Data is available on file.
ISBN: 978-1-61608-093-8

Printed in China

This book is dedicated to my late nephew
Shannon, who lived life to the fullest, partied
harder than was wise, and died far too young;
he was the Celtic warrior he always wanted to be.

Contents

GROWING MARIJUANA

> When you smoke the herb,
> it reveals you to yourself.
>
> —BOB MARLEY

Introduction

I'm writing this book because I believe that this excessively stressed-out world needs a straightforward, no-nonsense guide to growing small-area plots of high-grade marijuana for personal use. Recent years have seen a general relaxation of governmental prejudice toward the possession and use of marijuana, and although pot is at this time still a controlled drug in most places, it doesn't seem foolishly optimistic to hope that it will soon be decriminalized across the board.

Why This Book?
- Simple and direct instructions
- Guidelines are written specifically for small-scale growers
- Skills to either start from scratch or update your current techniques to grow a better yield

For today's enlightened citizens the real question is why this plant, which has been smoked and eaten for recreational purposes for at least 9,000 years, which has never harmed anyone physically or mentally, and which is virtually impossible to overdose on, should have been added to the FDA's list of Schedule I controlled substances (1970) in the first place. To place marijuana in the same criminal class as PCP and methadone is just wrong, and it's high time America stopped imprisoning its citizens for merely smoking a dead plant that anyone can grow.

I also believe strongly that what is not needed is another marijuana grower's guide that attempts to make the cultivation process so scientifically precise that it becomes an overcomplicated science experiment. For some growers, that's part of the fun of growing pot—making the activity into a hobby—but not here. Growing your own pot doesn't have to be just another labor in your already too-busy life; it should be an enjoyable and satisfying experience, watching living sprouts erupt from seeds that you've selected and sown yourself, nurturing vulnerable seedlings until they become stout and strong, and enjoying the fruits of your own handiwork. Raising marijuana shouldn't be another stress factor in your life, it should be a pleasure and a release from daily tensions.

It is my intent that this book keep it simple and keep it real, because the goal of the following chapters is to make anyone who wants to be one into a successful small pot farmer. As serious (a few are even obsessed) indoor and "closet" growers can attest, raising pot can be every bit as expensive as a person might want to make it, and as labor-intensive as a legal cash crop. High-pressure sodium lamps that approximate sunlight cost hundreds of dollars to buy, hundreds of dollars a year to run, and can pose a fire hazard; CO_2 tanks that help to keep enclosed indoor crops in roughly the plant equivalent of a hyperbaric chamber; even soilless hydroponic trays that grow plants rooted in foam and fed by nutrient-enriched water that is sometimes circulated and filtered using electric pumps to keep algae from growing: these are just some of the high-dollar items that can take a large bite out of whatever money a smoker might save by growing his own pot.

But growing a personal-use crop that will provide at least 1 ounce of cleaned, seedless, and stem-free buds for each month of the year (from harvest to harvest) doesn't have to require a lot of dedication or expense. (There will be some sweat involved, though, never doubt that.) Aside from a little fertilizer and a sackful of seeds, probably most growers who live south of the U.S. border with Mexico, and who rely on the pittance they're paid for their crops by smugglers who enjoy the real profits, have little money to reinvest into their farming operations.

Yet in spite of being cultivated under almost third-world conditions, "commercial" marijuana from Mexico and South America has dominated the black market in the United States for decades, because the simple farmers there understand the plants they cultivate. They've learned to exploit whatever advantages might be provided by a given

At the time of this writing, smokers' cafés like this one are still uncommon in the United States, but times are changing.

environment, be it a mountain glade, rainforest clearing, or low desert, to give plants what they need to achieve maximum growth.

That same philosophy is applicable to almost any growing zone, even those with short warm seasons—like where I live. It's no coincidence that some very good pot is coming from growers in western Canada who have learned to maximize their harvest within the limitations of a short, relatively cool growing period. Certainly there are pot-growing geniuses (I can't help envisioning the lab-coated schizophrenic cannabis expert in the Cheech and Chong movie *Nice Dreams*), and there are often sophisticated techniques for coaxing the most out of specific strains, but the fact is that all cannabis plants produce THC. It's also true that a grower doesn't need to have a degree in botany, a lot of money, or even a subscription to a marijuana magazine to grow a crop of buds that will keep him or her—and a few select friends—high until next year's harvest.

Smoked by people on either (or any) side of the political aisle, marijuana has become an icon of resistance to governmental control of American life.

Smoked by people on either (or any) side of the political aisle, marijuana has become an icon of resistance to governmental control of American life.

That isn't to say that anyone who wants to study which light wavelengths most benefit cannabis, and maybe buy lights that emit just the desired spectrum for a closet crop of manipulated plants grown under rigidly controlled conditions shouldn't get as far into the science of growing cannabis as he or she wants. But I believe that for beginners—and a few old hands, too—it's more edifying and more fun to first focus on just growing yourself a fine, healthy crop of cannabis with naturally big and fragrant buds that you can smugly get all of your friends stoned on. No grower I know has ever produced buds that wouldn't get a person high, and if plants are pruned just right, even the summer leaves can give you case of red-eye.

In that vein, the following chapters cater to the small farmer who doesn't sow acres of impersonal hemp for sale to the faceless public, but rears a few prized and pampered plants for his or her own serenity through a coming winter. (I throw one heck of a New Year's party, with whiskey glasses filled with joints, free to any guest in need of a buzz.) One readily apparent advantage that a small personal-use grower enjoys over large for-profit operations is more time to lavish personal attention on individual plants. For you, the small grower, the advantage of having fewer plants that can receive more personal care will become obvious as you follow the simplified guidelines presented in this book. Before long you won't be able to not notice that marijuana plants seized by police and shown on the evening news look frail and sparse in comparison to your own lush and robust plants. As you can see from the seed-to-harvest progression of photos depicting the crop that is shown throughout the book, a few well-tended plants can be made to grow thick and bushy, producing—as in this crop—as much as 2 ounces of bud per plant.

Because marijuana hasn't yet been completely legalized— and because I feel that whether you smoke pot, drink alcohol, or hang out in a sweat lodge, the experience is your own—this book doesn't bear my real name. Not because of any sense of shame—to the contrary, I've always wanted to write about the successes and failures of pot-growing endeavors that I've experienced personally or vicariously. The moniker

At the price of good marijuana on today's market—and with assistance from relaxed laws governing it—growing your own medicinal or recreational cannabis can be as financially sound as it is relaxing and satisfying.

American legislators have softened their stance on marijuana, and many states have legalized the plant for medical use.

Tommy McCarthy is one more layer of protection between drug enforcement agencies who are even now struggling to justify their more-than ample budgets and the many fine growers, smokers, and friends who have contributed so much to making this book possible. Maybe responsible, law-abiding citizens who have been made into criminals not by crimes they've committed but by government decree can soon stop worrying that a sandwich bag partially filled with dried weeds can cost them their homes and careers, their freedom, and even their children.

Life Cycle of Marijuana Plants

As a healthy marijuana plant thrives, it should hit several stages of growth on its way from seed to weed. Knowing what these milestones are before you start will give you an idea of what to expect as you cultivate your crop. Ultimately, marijuana plants are living objects—they are as susceptible to chance and change as the rest of us. There are no foolproof guidelines that can guarantee you the best product ever. Even if you follow every suggestion in this book to the letter, some plants simply might not thrive. It happens. That being said, humans have been cultivating marijuana for a couple of thousand years now, and knowing what to expect as you grow will help you assess and deal with any speed bumps you may hit along the way.

Inactive Seeds—All marijuana grows from single seeds produced by two parent plants that have reproduced "sexually"—meaning the seed contains genes from both a male and female "parent" plant. (Note: there are hermaphroditic plants that produce seeds without a partner, but this phenomenon is rare and fairly inconsequential for small growers.) Seeds are dormant until activated by exposure to water and light. Until this happens they are fairly hardy. The biggest danger tends to come from extremely low temperatures—anything below 20°F will kill a seed.

Sprouting Stage (also known as "Germination")—Once a seed is exposed to light and moisture, a series of hormones within the seed activate the growing process itself (for information on "sprouting," see **Chapter Four**). A single root will split the outer shell of the seed and grow downward in order to cull water and nutrients from the surrounding environment. Almost simultaneously, a green stalk will reach upward, and two round "cotyledon" leaves will appear above the soil. Germination can usually be triggered in a number of ways, several of which are discussed later in this book, and a healthy seed should take no more than seven days to germinate fully.

Seedling State—For healthy plants, it will usually take three to seven days for a "sprout" to officially enter the "seedling" stage. This period of growth is defined by the establishment of a small yet stable root system, as well as the appearance of "true leaves" on your small plant. "True leaves" are green leaves that have the distinct shape exhibited by mature marijuana leaves—as opposed to the generic looking and round "cotyledon" leaves that first grew above the soil.

The seedling stage can last anywhere from three to six weeks, although variations may occur due to over- or underwatering. The general rule of thumb for seedlings is that they require a small but steady supply of water. As your seedlings grow, you will need to pay attention to the rate at which foliage begins to appear. After a stable root system has been established, the plant will begin to focus on chlorophyll production and begin to move into the next stage of growth, known as the "vegetative" state. (This transition from "seedling" to "vegetative" plant is particularly important for deciding when to transplant your crop. See **Chapter Five** for more details.)

Vegetative State—One of the most rewarding and critical periods of plant growth, the "vegetative" state occurs when a marijuana plant begins to produce large, green leaves at a rapid rate. This flourish of foliage is a direct result of an increased capacity for the marijuana plant to absorb and process nutrients and CO_2. During this period, the root system will continue to expand outward while vertical height increases. Healthy plants can grow as much as 1½ to 2 inches a day during the vegetative state.

Because marijuana plant cycles are triggered by changes in light (this characteristic is known as "photoperiodic-reactive"), it is possible for a grower to keep a plant in a permanent vegetative state. To do so, a person must carefully control the amount of light that shines in the growing environment. For growers who choose to plant outdoors and rely on nature for sunlight, the length of the vegetative state will vary depending on location. However, no matter where a grower plants, marijuana will begin to show distinctive gender characteristics usually around the fourth week of vegetative growth (for more information regarding plant gender and identification, see **Chapters One** and **Eight**).

Flowering State—Ultimately, this final stage of the marijuana life cycle is the most important for growers and smokers alike. The "flowering" state occurs in both male and female plants when an individual plant is sexually mature and ready to reproduce. (Note: though this stage occurs in both male and female plants, it occurs at different times depending on gender. Generally, male plants will reach the flowering stage one to two weeks before their female counterparts.)

When a marijuana plant reaches sexual maturity, it begins to produce massive amounts of resin that appears on the outside of leaves. This sticky resin is highly concentrated on and around the reproductive organs of the plant (these organs are popularly referred to as the "buds" of the plant), and it contains tetrahydrocannibinol (THC)—the active intoxicating ingredient in marijuana. When looked at closely, the resin on a plant in the flowering stage will actually appear to be covered in tiny clear (and milky white) protrusions. These are called "trichomes." The potency of the THC in these protrusions will vary depending on how long an individual plant has been in the flowering stage and whether the plant has been fertilized or not.

Ultimately, the purpose of growing your own pot is to harvest these buds, dry them, and smoke the best pot money didn't have to buy. However, the question of when to harvest is significant enough to warrant its own chapter later on this book. For now, it's important to understand that the length of the flowering stage can vary depending on what cannabis strain you're working with and how much control you have over your growing environment. Most strains of cannabis flower for six to ten weeks (although a few have been known to flourish for up to four months under ideal conditions).

PART ONE

Supplies and What to Consider before You Start—

BASIC BACKGROUND INFORMATION ON SEEDS, SOIL, AND FERTILIZER

CHAPTER 1

Seeds

Step One: **Before you plant, you need to plan. This chapter will introduce you to the basic information you need to decide what type of plant you want to grow.**

Growing marijuana plants that deliver maximum potency and volume from a minimum number of plants is a series of steps, each of which must be accomplished with some degree of success if a harvest is to be all that it can be. Or if it is to be at all; in my early years, when I was learning the hard way and sorting between sometimes utter nonsense and good, usable advice, there were more than a few years when I was just plain skunked, with not a single sprout surviving to maturity. That hasn't happened to me in a decade or so, but personal observations tell me that it happens more often than not with most beginners, until a lot of them just stop trying to grow cannabis and buy it instead.

Focus Points:
- **What Kind of Plant Do You Want to Grow: Male vs. Female**
- **Pick Your Strain: Hemp and Two Breeds of Marijuana**
- **Selecting Seeds: Quality and Characteristics**
- **Where to Buy: Commercial Seed Sources**

It doesn't help that cannabis growers have always had to hide their work, but impatience is a problem within today's instant-gratification society—made that way by computers, microwave ovens, and a multitude of modern conveniences. Today only a few farmers and gardeners still enjoy the experience of helping to create and nurture living things the way almost every American did just three or four generations ago.

As you start your own project, understand that no step in the growing process holds more importance than the seeds from which your crop will grow. Good seeds cannot by themselves guarantee that you'll enjoy a bountiful harvest, but seeds that germinate into healthy, vibrant sprouts as soon as they emerge and grow energetically are always preferred. The best seeds can produce plants that are more hardy and more adaptable to various conditions, and they can in a real sense extend the active growing season by producing foliage as quickly as possible, making the most of every day, and growing the biggest buds in the shortest time.

What Kind of Plant Do You Want to Grow: Male vs. Female

Seeds for marijuana plants are sold as either **male** or **female** in gender. This distinction is based on the fact that mature plants either pollinate (male) or ovulate (female) seeds for the next generation of plants. There can be hermaphrodite plants with both male and female organs, but for the most part you're going to be buying seeds sold as either one or the other.

The gender of a plant will become more important later on in your project as you get closer to harvesting. But for now, just remember that gender is important because different characteristics will manifest in adult plants based on their individual sex.

There are companies (most of them in Holland, all of them online) that market selectively bred and manipulated "feminized" seeds that they promise will grow giant female plants with giant chronic buds. These superseeds, often individually blister-packed and sold for more than a dollar each, are shipped in a plain brown envelope with no markings—although possession of marijuana seeds is not itself illegal in most places. Sources for seeds are given at the back of this book.

Pick Your Strain: Hemp and Two Breeds of Marijuana

Cannabis has been grown to smoke or eat for medicinal purposes, and for the purpose of altering its users' perception of the world around him since at least 2800 BC, according to the United States Department of Agriculture (7000 BC if you believe some accredited authorities on marijuana).

The USDA lumps all varieties of THC-producing plants under the common genus name *Cannabis.* Under that title, the agency lists just two subtypes of cannabis: hemp and marijuana.

Hemp

Hemp (*Cannabis ruderalis*), which they call "ditchweed," is a subspecies defined by its commercially valuable rope fiber derived from mature male plant stems. Hemp was a cash crop in America until passage of the 1937 Marihuana Tax Act, partially because ditchweed can grow wild in climates where winter doesn't freeze the soil and kill the seeds. According to the USDA, "ditchweed" has a low THC content and isn't worth smoking. You can tell that the experts who drafted that report aren't pot growers; judicious pruning is a technique that I've always used to increase plants' THC content. (My theory is that, like the oils produced by catnip and other mint leaves, THC is an insect repellant whose concentration is increased within a plant's tissues in response to a perceived attack.) A plant that grows to maturity unattended will produce the flowers or buds of its gender, but if it has not been eaten by insects—or judiciously pruned—just enough to make it grow stronger, but without retarding its growth, its buds will be seedy and probably not very potent. Cannabis growing in a highway ditch in southern Indiana, for example, has ideal conditions under which to shoot up tall and maximize the distance over which pollen and seeds can spread, and is probably in little danger from plant eaters. It will grow tall and strong, but it won't produce a lot of branches that would in turn sprout a lot of leaves and buds, and it will have little or no need to protect itself from predation by increasing levels of THC within its tissues. But if the same so-called ditchweed were to grow from sprout to maturity with careful pruning, plenty of water, and an occasional feeding, it would grow bushy and yield potent smoke.

Chapter 8 offers more detailed information regarding the process of identifying your plants' genders. However, familiarizing yourself with a few of the male and female characteristics now will help you make more informed purchasing decisions when you look for seeds.

Male Plants:

- Generally taller with less bushy structure
- Lower THC production compared to females
- Reproductive structures mature earlier than their female counterparts. These organs first appear as a small appendage protruding from the stalk at the juncture where a new branch is forming. As the plant matures these organs turn into green-white egg-shaped flowers called pollen sacks. Once open, pollen-coated stamens hang down from these sacks. Gravity helps distribute the pollen on smaller, female plants, growing below the males.

Female Plants

- Shorter and bushier than male counterparts
- Higher THC production (especially during flowering state)
- Reproductive structures first appear as bumps coming off the main stalk at the juncture where new leaves form. These bumps (called the calyx) develop a raindrop shape. Two fuzzy hairs (pistils) grow from the top of each calyx and form a "V" shape. As the flowering phase continues more pistils will sprout from each calyx. Eventually, these clustered groups become the prized "buds" of the female plant.

Marijuana

The other type of cannabis recognized by the U.S. government is what has been legally defined as "marihuana," which was effectively outlawed by the catch-22 Marihuana Tax Act of 1937, and which has for more than four decades been classed in the same legal category as crack, PCP, and heroin. Native all over the world in one subspecies or another, cannabis was grown for use as marijuana by George Washington, Thomas Jefferson, and Benjamin Franklin, to name a few of the great minds who smoked pot. It was a staple medicinal and recreational drug already known to most immigrants who came to the New World from Asia, India, China, and Africa.

Within the larger "marijuana" classification, there are several different types of species, but for the purposes of this book, growers should be concerned with the two largest categories of "marijuana" strains on the market: *Cannabis indica* and *Cannabis sativa*. Individual breeders and growers might offer several different species of marijuana, but most of these actually fall within the larger *indica* and *sativa* groups (for example, only a select few breeders will distinguish *Cannabis afghanica* from the umbrella *indica* strain to which it belongs).

Cannabis indica

Indica origins come from countries including Tibet, Afghanistan, Kashmir, and Morocco, countries in which hash (a THC-containing paste made from refining marijuana leaves) and kif (a THC-containing

This drawing depicts both male and female reproductive structures. The hanging male pollen sacks can be seen in the lower left corner, and the female calyx with two rising pistils can be seen in the bottom right corner.

Prejudices being what they were in the early 1900s, cannabis became associated with immigrants of non-Caucasian persuasion, and the plant also fell victim to racism. California was first to outlaw marijuana in 1913, because it was widely believed that the growing number of white kids who were partaking of marijuana were being negatively influenced by lower-caste minorities who cultivated it. That was intolerable in genteel circles, so politicians tried to placate their favorite campaign contributors in the only way they can, by legislating marijuana out of existence.

That obviously didn't work—never has. An insatiable demand—spurred by rebelliousness, because Americans traditionally don't take well to being ruled—and sometimes obscene profit margins created a new frontier for high-tech botanist-growers. By the mid-1970s you could buy a bag of buds with names like Acapulco Gold, Maui Wowie, and Sinsemilla, and the race to create new strains was on. Today there are enough strains of recreational and medicinal cannabis to fill a photo album, with a diversity of mental effects, and even taste and smell, to suit different tastes and moods.

powder also made from marijuana) production are a longtime tradition. *Indicas* are usually short plants between 3 and 6 feet tall, with broad leaves and often dense foliage that is dark green-blue, sometimes tinged with purple. As the *indica* plant matures, its leaves may become significantly more purple, and the buds may be thick and dense. *Indica* are strong-smelling plants with a "skunky" taste and smell. The smoke from an *indica* is generally a body type stone, hypnotic and relaxing. Better known *indica* strains include Afghan, Durban Poison, Skunk, Papaya, and Hindu Kush.

Cannabis sativa

Sativas are originally from Mexico, Southeast Asia, Thailand, and Colombia, but although they originated in a tropical environment, plants have proved to be very tough in cold weather, surviving even when covered with snow. *Sativa* plants are tall and slender, generally between 8 and 12 feet. You might say that a *sativa* is the opposite of an *indica*, being thin, with narrower leaves than an *indica*, and a lighter green color. A *sativa* bud becomes red as it matures in a warm environment and can turn to purple if it matures in a colder environment. Some *sativa* varieties can even have yellow ("gold") pigments. *Sativa* plants have a pleasantly spicy, sweet, and fruity smell, if cured properly, and the high is cerebral and energetic, almost amphetamine-like. Popular *sativa* strains are California Orange Bud, Ice, Super Ice, New Purple Power, Swazi, Jock Horror, and Maui Waui.

Selecting Seeds: Quality and Characteristics

Now that you have an idea of what strain you want to grow, you want to make sure you know what to look for when buying this most important seed supply. Examining your seeds and checking your product is the best way to avoid a wasted growing season due to a skunked crop.

This beautiful female *sativa* is almost in full bloom.

More experienced growers may want a variety of male and female plants, but the danger here lies in uncontrolled fertilization. Unfertilized female plants tend to produce bigger and more potent buds. Fertilized females will provide you with materials for next year's crop, but the buds will be smaller and filled with seeds. The labor and planning required for multigenerational breeding is beyond the scope of this book, so for the sake of just getting your feet wet, feel free to go for commercially sold "feminized" seeds from a producer (for more information on seed production, see **Chapter Eight**).

Probably most home growers will begin their first crops by culling the seeds they sow from commercially purchased bags of marijuana. Be warned that imported pot from often-sophisticated outlaw factories is processed and packaged in large quantities that may exceed 1,000 pounds per harvest. Budded mature plants are hung upside down in open-air sheds until they've dried to a tacky texture, and have a predetermined moisture content that may be monitored by digital humidity gauges. When plants are cured to the desired level, bud-bearing stems are snipped from the main stem and stuffed into vacuum-seal bags, 1 pound or 1 kilogram per bag. Vacuum-sealed bags are subjected to all manner of rough handling—and exposure to environments and materials that would certainly be restricted by the Food and Drug Administration if marijuana were sold legally.

It's worth the time it takes to inspect your seeds. Knowing how many seeds you expect to germinate will also help you plan expenses as you go buy potting soil, peat plugs, and other equipment.

These fresh seeds have just been culled from a fully harvested crop. As your project progresses you will have to decide if you want to let a few plants produce their own seeds for next year's plants.

What all this has to do with culling seeds for growing from black-market pot sold on the street is less than good. Many seeds are immature when the parent plant is harvested, because there's just no time for large-scale pot farmers to ensure that each branch gets all the sunlight it needs to produce maximum-size buds and robust seeds. In fact, it is only because the task of culling seeds from large quantities of marijuana is such a daunting task that end users can expect to find any seeds at all in a bag—remember, it isn't in the best interest of professional growers to encourage do-it-yourselfers. So don't be disappointed to find seeds that have been crushed during vacuum-sealing or rough handling. Less obvious are seeds that have been frozen; cannabis is not native to latitudes where winter covers the earth with snow for several months of each year, and seeds that are frozen are unlikely to reproduce.

It has been estimated that just one out of three pot seeds will actually sprout. What this arbitrary statement really means is that many of the seeds growers plant won't sprout for a number of reasons. These include immature seeds, seeds whose husks have been cracked to expose the vulnerable germ inside, and seeds that have been killed by extremes of cold, heat, dryness, or time.

It is possible to cull seeds to save only the best, most likely to succeed candidates and increase the sprouting rate to nearly 100 percent. **Mature seeds are not whitish or light green, but dark brown, often with a marbling of lighter stripes. Among these, the best choices are fat, round seeds.** Smaller, unmarbled brown seeds may sprout and grow well, too, but in general, the healthier and better developed the seed, the stronger the sprout.

On "buds" (the protruding organ that facilitates reproduction in marijuana plants), seeds grow directly from and very close to their parent stems. They're usually out of sight under an insulating layer of bud material and protected from the crushing forces of baling and vacuum-sealing by their woody stems—that's why many survive to reach

Different characteristics of the various strains do not manifest until plants are fully mature. Your grab bag of seeds will all pretty much look the same.

UGA1459313

Be aware—especially if you're a closet grower—that feminized seeds produce only female plants, and if you plant a crop of all females with no males around to pollinate them, they will produce few or no seeds. The drawback for a personal-use grower who relies on harvesting seeds for the next crop from one autumn to the next is that there will be no seeds unless he or she can also plant a few nonfeminized seeds, at least half of which will be flowering males. In fact, I recommend this, because if a cannabis strain is especially nice to smoke or eat, you'll probably want to carry on those qualities in next year's crop (for more information on plant reproduction, see **Chapters Eight** and **Nine**).

end users in intact and plantable condition (for more information on buds, see **Chapter Eight**). Green seeds are sheathed in a protective green-white cellulose envelope that falls away as a seed darkens in maturity. With green or dry buds, the easiest method of removing seeds for sowing is to locate them, then gently roll them free of their stems using a thumbnail. Discard any with cracked or broken hulls and those with whitish, unmatured hulls.

Where to Buy: Commercial Seed Sources

The crop shown in upcoming chapters was grown specifically for this grower's guide and is a product of "mongrel" seeds culled from a half-ounce of marijuana purchased from a dealer. However, if the seeds from your last purchase are in too poor a condition to plant, there are a number of hemp seed suppliers around the world. Mailed in plain brown blister-padded envelopes that give no indication of their contents, these hand-picked "feminized" seeds have been harvested from plants selectively bred to grow fast, strong, and large. It is an almost suspicious legal irony that most states (and countries) have no laws against the possession of cannabis seeds, and they do not become a controlled substance until you plant them.

Often priced at well over U.S. $1 per seed, these highly manipulated designer breeds promise to be of unique, highly specialized strains, all claimed to provide a different type of high. The buds of some are exotic looking, very different from natural *indicas*

and *sativas*, and all of them have been selectively bred to produce the largest buds possible. At this time, typing "cannabis seeds" into an Internet search engine will net more seed sellers than most growers will want to sort through.

I'm an uncultured swine when it comes to pot, and I frequently fail to appreciate the subtle nuances of designer-weed highs; all I care about is that it gets me as stoned as I'd like to be for as long as I'd like to be, and with as few tokes as possible. The bottom line is that virtually all cultivated, tended, and properly cured buds will get the most hardened smoker high. If your budget permits paying as much for each seed as you would for a can of soda, and you want to try growing plants with big buds and names like Durban Poison and White Widow, by all means give them a try; you probably won't be disappointed with the results.

Soil

***Step Two**:* **Once you have your seeds, the next step is to ensure your plant gets off to the best possible start. Preparing the best soil and buying the right equipment are the crucial next steps in developing an awesome crop.**

Note to the reader: Numerous growers across the globe choose to cultivate their product in hydroponic garden systems. Because marijuana plants can use nutrients as soon as they are absorbed, cannabis often grows extremely fast in hydroponic gardens. However, the time, equipment, and skill required to successfully maintain a hydro system is far beyond the scope and goals of this book (see Chapter Five for more details). Ultimately, the best way to be a single, self-sufficient grower is to go back to basics—pick up your seeds and get ready to get your hands dirty.

Focus Points:
- **The Importance of Soil**
- **Soils That Work: Store Supplies and Cutting Your Dirt**
- **Making Your Own Soil**
- **Changing the Soil of Your Grow Plot**

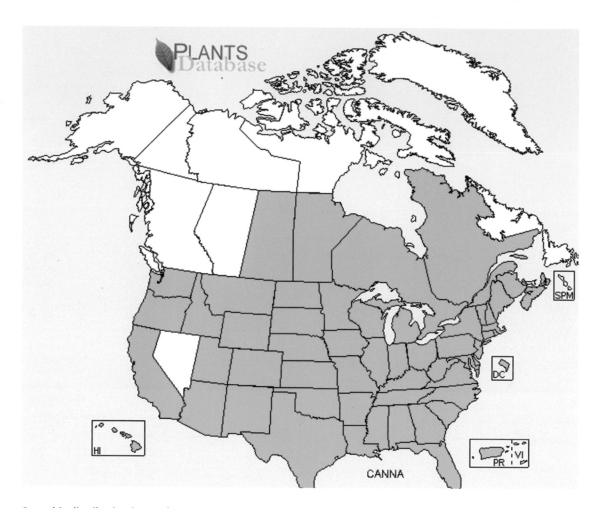

Cannabis distribution in North America (courtesy USDA).

The Importance of Soil

To a plant, soil is a good portion of the world. Soil provides a good anchor against high winds and pounding rain. Soil carries water to thirsty roots, which also absorb nutrients that enable a plant to grow strong. A good soil absorbs several times its own weight in water and holds that water like a sponge, keeping it available to your plants' root systems for as long as possible before evaporating. A good soil remains loose, whether wet or dry, with enough density to allow roots to gain a strong grip, but airy enough to permit easy expansion of nutrient-absorbing root tendrils as they spread to accommodate a

One particular way of reproducing a plant is known as "cloning." Cloning involves cutting off a piece of greenery from a nonflowering "mother plant" and then replanting the fragile leaflet in a separate pot. Though this process is described in further detail in chapter 9, it is important to get in the habit of paying attention to soil composition early on in your growing experiment.

growing plant's needs. Conversely, a poor soil can hamper your plants' growth and cause them to be stunted, or even just prevent them from achieving their full potential, so it pays to start with the best soil you can get.

Ultimately, whether you decided to mature your plant indoors or outside, soil is going to be a key ingredient in your success. If you're following the suggested order of this book, then you're going to grow your plant from its most infantile stage as a seed up through mature harvesting. If you're working with a cutting or already have a small plant, eventually your greenery is going to outgrow its current home, and soil is going to be a primary concern when repotting.

A healthy cannabis plant proper soil is essential to every stage of development.

As you grow your crop, your plants are going to go through several different stages in their life cycle (see "Marijuana Life Cycle" section provided in the beginning of this book). The supplies needed for growth will change depending on how old your plant is. The next section of this chapter contains information that will help you decide what equipment you need for the initial "sprouting" of your seeds (the stage where you trigger the growth process itself). Beyond this stage, you will want to consider the best soil type for your plant once it's ready to be placed in a permanent container. For information regarding the actual process of growing your plant, refer to part 2 of t his book.

Soils That Work: Store Supplies and Cutting Your Dirt

Peat plugs are probably the simplest and most convenient starting media. These mesh-covered cylinders of dried sphagnum moss are a good choice for starting most types of plants from seeds. They can be found at any home garden and supply store and usually come with a small terrarium top and shallow tray for easy storage.

To get started simply indent a small hole, half an inch deep, into the top of the plug using a pencil, drop in one or two seeds, and set the sown peat plugs into the

The ground around these healthy marijuana plants is obviously poor, and no one would expect to find them thriving in such a place.

tray. Add a half an inch of water to cover the bottom. Peat plugs readily absorb water, keeping seeds on their tops exposed to the moisture needed to make them sprout, but they also radiate moisture rapidly through evaporation, so be sure to keep sown plugs well watered.

If you are not able to find peat plugs, potting soil is a readily available and inexpensive seed starter that might be found anywhere from the garden center at Walmart to grocery stores. Both potting soil and the similar (but usually more expensive) composted manure are rich in the nutrients needed to nourish sprouts of most species into strong and vigorous seedlings. Just gently press a seed about halfway down into the soil, and then keep the soil moist and soft at all times, because ultradense potting soil becomes hard as mortar if allowed to dry, quickly strangling plants rooted in it.

Marijuana growers and gardeners alike tend to "cut" store-bought potting soil with sand or whatever local soil might be available. A mix of fifty-fifty that blends potting soil with leaf or grass mulch, dried sphagnum (peat) moss, or almost any local dirt or sand that will grow a plant provides more than enough nutrition for the first critical stages of growth, so a sack of potting soil can cover twice as much. More importantly, the addition of nonclumping media prevents potting soil from hardening, which is critical to the unrestricted expansion of roots as a growing plant seeks more nutrition, water, and a stronger grip on the earth.

Making Your Own Soil

If you live on or near a farm, or if you're willing to compost your own rich growing soil from animal scat and other organics, you can create your own highly effective soil (see **Chapter Three**). Cow and especially pig excrement mucked out from stalls and sties, then aged a year or more, is an outstanding growing

Specialty soils like these help to make growing cannabis—or any plant—easier than it has ever been.

Better than "knee-high by the Fourth of July," these vibrant midsummer plants show what good soil can do in the poorest environment.

medium, even when mixed half-and-half with sand. Also look to excavation companies that collect topsoil from job sites and often sell it cheaply by the pickup load; good black topsoil can be used for starting healthy marijuana plants as-is.

Changing the Soil of Your Grow Plot

Even after your seeds have successfully sprouted, soil quality can have a serious impact on the life cycle of maturing marijuana. If you choose to grow exclusively indoors your ability to control the soil quality increases tremendously. However, if you decide to sow your product outdoors, you can use rich ready-made soil to create an oasis of healthy growth in places where marijuana couldn't grow by itself. That has been exploited to good advantage by generations of outlaw pot farmers who use this "oasis method" to create small, hard-to-see plots of thriving hemp plants in environments where drug cops wouldn't expect to find them growing and in terrain where most intrepid outdoorspeople won't stumble onto them.

No two ideal growing spots will be the same, but most soils can be made to support cannabis plants with the judicious application of plain old plant food and fertilizer (see **Chapter Three**).

CHAPTER 3

Fertilizer

Step Three: **Picking the right fertilizer can make the difference between a plant that is merely "surviving" and a plant that is truly "thriving." Before you start growing, you want to know what your plant will need throughout its life cycle and how to buy (or create) your own plant food supplies.**

Focus Points:
- **What Cannabis Plants Eat**
- **The Science Behind the Food**
- **Popular Choices for Effective Fertilizer**
- **Composting**
- **Note for Indoor Growers**

Fertilizer, generally, is any element that can be introduced to soil, water, or to a plant itself that will spur healthy growth beyond what it would be without aid from the fertilizing element. Just as a human athlete needs a proper diet to achieve maximum performance levels, so does a cultivated plant require the equivalent of a healthy diet to attain maximum growth. There are many types and forms of fertilizer, but the one that works best is the one that most effectively provides the health-enhancing nutrients that a plant needs most at that time. For now, for our purposes, forget sophisticated and often expensive soil and water testers; you can do very well using only a few proven basics and simple off-the-shelf growing products.

What Cannabis Plants Eat

The three main elements marijuana plants need are nitrogen (N), phosphorus (P), and potassium (K). All three of these are needed for strong root growth, vigorous leafing, and for lush flowers with high yields. Commercial potting soils are preblended with a balanced NPK ratio that will sustain a plant for the first two or three weeks. As plants grow taller and broader, supplemental nutrients are required.

When deciding what to feed your plant and how much to provide, refer back to the "Marijuana Life Cycle" section provided at the beginning of this book.

Once you reach the vegetative, or leafing, stage, a good "20–20–20" supplement is often adequate to maintain proper growth and development; that designation stands for the percentage of nitrogen, phosphorous, and potassium infused into potting soil when it is manufactured. Indoor growers dilute this formula to one-half or one-quarter strength, because enclosed marijuana does not tolerate full-strength nutrient feedings well, and may exhibit the leaf drooping associated with a temporary shock to the system. Diluted solutions of 20 percent NPK are probably best administered twice a week, although some growers feed their plants at every watering. Marijuana plants grown outdoors aren't so finicky, perhaps because they have greater freedom for root growth and breathe naturally fresh air.

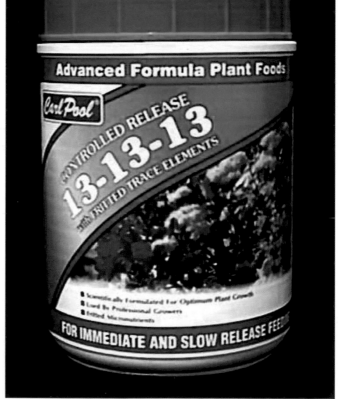

The designator "13–13–13" on this jar of plant food indicates an NPK content of 13 percent nitrogen (N), 13 percent phosphorous (P), and 13 percent potassium (K).

The Science Behind the Food

Just as in people and animals, all of the nutrients listed here work together to maintain healthy growth and development, and every one of them can be critical. Plants may grow poorly, refuse to grow at all, or even die if deprived of any one of these nutrients, because some are symbiotic in their ability to be metabolized as food. If deprivation is acute, a plant may go into "nutrient lockout," a phenomenon in which the lack of a single necessary element disables the plant's ability to absorb some or all of the other nutritional elements. When deciding which fertilizer you want to use, pay attention to the ingredients you see on the side of the box. You don't need to understand the exact bioscience behind the numerous chemical ingredients in each product, but if you know what elements to look for, you stand a better chance of providing the best munchies for your hungry plant.

Plant food tablets, and the similar fertilizer spikes, dissolve slowly into the surrounding soil, helping to keep it and the plants supported by that soil from becoming depleted of necessary nutrients as the needs of growing plants change.

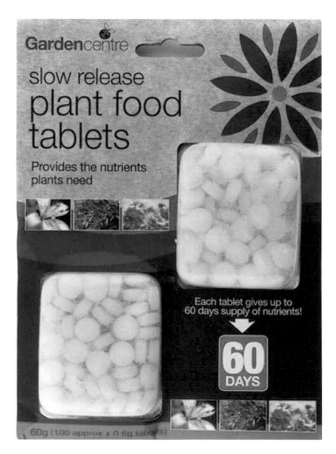

- In the flowering stage, an increased amount of phosphorus is needed to promote the production of flowers and bud sites and to encourage maximum yield. Phosphorus by itself, or in a higher, unbalanced ratio of 10–30–10 (10 percent nitrogen, 30 percent phosphorous, and 10 percent potassium), is the most preferred feeding mix at this stage.
- Secondary foods that are required to achieve maximum growth and potency include calcium (Ca), sulphur (S), and magnesium (Mg). These nutritional elements ensure that plant photosynthesis will be at peak efficiency, inducing strong growth and rapid development.
- Trace minerals a plant needs include boron (B), copper (Cu), molybdenum (Mo), zinc (Zn), iron (Fe), and manganese (Mn). Only small amounts of these elements are needed, but they are essential parts of the formula for total health.

Health problems that your plants experience as a result of needing nutrients are easy to remedy with almost any off-the-shelf general-purpose plant food, but you must act quickly (see **Chapter Seven**, Hazards to Your Plants, for more information). Aside from the need to bring a plant back to verdant health, think in terms of lost growth; a healthy plant in mid-July is typically between 2 and 3 feet tall, and before harvesttime in October or November it will be 5 feet tall or more. Even a mild case of plant malnutrition can subtract two weeks of potential growth, so it's important to keep plants as healthy as they can possibly be throughout their growing cycle.

Popular Choices for Effective Fertilizer

Vermiculite and Perlite

Vermiculite and Perlite are two commercial pellet-type fertilizers made by heating mica to 1,400 degrees F. and 1,800 degrees F., respectively. The heating process causes the minerals to expand and become porous; the resulting white pellets can absorb water up to four times their own weight in water, they hold air, and they keep dense potting soils from hardening into solid masses when they dry. The mineral itself provides potassium, magnesium, and calcium that leaches into soil over time to nourish roots. Pellets of either fertilizer are further enhanced by saturating them with a combination of nutrients that are also released over time.

For hydroponic growing, perlite or vermiculite is typically used in a high concentration of 50 percent fertilizer, with the remainder a combination of water and peat moss—proving that it is hard to overfertilize with either product. Soil growers can get by with a much smaller ratio of one part vermiculite or perlite per ten parts soil. Perlite and vermiculite are most commonly sold in 0.4 cubic-foot bags or 6 cubic-foot bales.

Miracle-Gro™, et al.

When it comes to home gardening fertilizers, it's tough to argue with a proven formula, and ready-made plant foods like Miracle-Gro have a long track record of success. I've watered my own cannabis plants with one or another brand of all-purpose plant food for decades, and the results have been satisfying enough to keep me using them. With them the engineering has already been done; all I have to do is mix and

Finding a plant food that's blended to meet your plants' specific needs is usually as simple as buying an off-the-shelf product.

apply as directed. Along with water-mixed powders and liquids, there are nontoxic leaf-feeding sprays that some growers like and some don't, because they may or may not affect how smoothly the cured plant smokes.

Urine

Stoners may recall a scene from the movie *Nice Dreams* in which Cheech complained to Chong that one of his plants was looking a little unhealthy. Chong's reply was "Piss on 'em."

There is sound science behind Tommy Chong's cryptic advice. Nitrogen is a booster to leaf and stem production and is critical to cannabis growth throughout the summer months. Almost as symbiotically, human urine is largely comprised of nitrogen urea, and it has served well for making pot plants thick with leaves for generations. The usual recipe is one bladderful per gallon of water, sometimes mixed with a commercial plant food. Do not urinate on the plants (unadulterated urine will probably kill where it touches, for one thing), or onto the ground near a plant; always dilute urine in a water solution, and use the solution promptly to prevent the formation of harmful ammonia.

Wood Ashes

Where I live, the surrounding forests are mostly conifers, and most of those are jack pines. As a result, the sandy soil below them has a very high acid content that can be tolerated by few plants other than blueberries and bracken ferns—even cannabis, which generally likes acidic soils, cannot grow here without assistance. One simple solution has been to deacidify the soil by adding a caustic (i.e., lye) that neutralizes acids. Lime from your local garden center is made for this task, but an old farmer's trick is to use plain wood ashes, blended in water at about one shovelful per 5-gallon bucket.

Carbon-dioxide generators

Probably every middle-school student knows that plants breathe in carbon dioxide, CO_2, and exhale oxygen, O_2, while animals breathe oxygen and exhale carbon dioxide. It's an ideal symbiotic relationship—or at least it was until Homo sapiens decided to pave everything. Just as human hospital patients experience faster recovery times when their lungs are superoxygenated, so can marijuana growth be accelerated in a CO_2-rich environment.

Vinegar-baking soda CO_2 generator

Probably the simplest carbon-dioxide generator is comprised of nothing more complicated than plain white vinegar dripping slowly—about one drop every two minutes is ideal—into a 1-liter bowl containing ordinary baking soda. The acidic vinegar combines with the caustic baking soda in a chemical reaction that not only renders both of those properties inert but also creates copious amounts of carbon dioxide until the vinegar runs out or the baking soda is entirely neutralized.

Closet growers generally set up their vinegar-soda CO_2 generators kind of like an intravenous (I.V.) drip used in hospitals. In its simplest form, a bottle filled with vinegar is duct-taped, hung, or otherwise suspended upside down over an open margarine container, or some other bowl, half-filled with baking soda. A hole punched through the vinegar bottle's cap using a finishing nail permits its contents to slowly drip from

Time-release liquid-drip individual plant feeders.

the hole and into the bowl of soda below. I like to extend a small-diameter oxygen-cannula hose from the hole in the vinegar's cap, sealing it on both sides with silicone caulk that will prevent the hole from sucking air and causing vinegar to drip too quickly. I like that the hose enables precisely directing where the vinegar drops will land.

CO_2 "bomb"

A vinegar-soda drip generator doesn't work well in the outdoors, where open breezes quickly carry off any CO_2 that is generated—along with a steady and unmistakable odor of vinegar that could, if the breeze was favorable, lead thieves or authorities directly to your plot.

For this type of generator to be useful it needs to swiftly generate an atmosphere rich in carbon dioxide within a small enclosed space that mostly or completely prohibits escape to the outside. A solution that has been useful consists of covering a plant entirely with a large plastic bag, the length of which is at least sufficient to reach the ground without bending over a plant's top. Next I place a plastic peanut butter jar or similar jar that is one-quarter filled with baking soda and place the open jar upright under the tent formed by the plastic bag. Then I reach under the bag's hem and pour a tablespoonful of vinegar into the jar until it begins to foam as it generates CO_2. Reseal the bag against the ground, let the plant breathe for fifteen minutes, then add more vinegar to the remaining baking soda, stirring the mix with a stick to ensure that all vinegar and soda have been combined. Leave the CO_2-filled bag over your plant for about four hours to thoroughly infuse its tissues, and repeat as you deem necessary.

You cannot give a plant too much CO_2, but I prefer to use bombs at night, when there are rarely people around to smell them. I also feel better about covering up my plants at night, when the process won't deny them vital sunlight.

Composting

I once used a mound of frequently turned-over five-year-old sled-dog poop to grow a thriving crop of thirty-three plants, of which twenty-two were females of several strains, with a harvest of 3 pounds of pretty excellent bud. Locals I spoke with were virtually unanimous in their opinion that husky turds would somehow fail to break

Liquid plant food is the author's favorite type, because it goes into solution immediately and thoroughly when mixed with water and is easy to transport afield to remote grow operations.

down, decay, and return to earth, like every other organic material does. But after five years the oldest end of the scat mound looked and smelled like rich, black dirt, and it grew one of the best marijuana crops that I've had the pleasure of harvesting.

Basically, if it's organic it will rot back into soil, taking whatever nutrients the original matter contained with it, available for infusion into the next plant. Composting kitchen waste and other organics normally results in an outstanding soil, and it can be accomplished in virtually any environment. Whether it be a heap in the woods 100 yards from your house or a covered 55-gallon drum on the roof of an apartment building, composting cuts down on a household's contribution to landfills and generates a good supply of rich soil for growing in habitats where native soil is poor—or nonexistent.

Once you've established a compost heap, begin another while the first is left alone to decompose. Frequently—daily, if possible—turn the compost with a pitchfork until the contents are well mixed. This helps to maxi- mize decomposition, to keep its progression even throughout the mass, and to minimize transition time from rotting organic to black dirt. Frequent turning also helps to prevent spontaneous combustion, a phenomenon in which heat generated by microbes feeding on damp, decaying material under pressure becomes sufficient to dry, then ignite the very material that created it. Soft tissues—tomatoes, old hamburger, gone-bad potatoes— rot the quickest and fastest in hot weather, but under ideal conditions, expect your compost heap to take at least three months to become usable soil.

Note for Indoor Growers

Having highlighted the importance of proper nutrition to growing a kick-ass crop, I must also point out that, like spider mites, malnutrition is most often seen in closet crops, where root and living space is confined. Just as natural predators and the elements keep spider mites under control in the wild, so does

runoff from rain bring in organic and mineral elements to periodically refresh the soil around in-ground pot plants. When you pull up your plants at harvest, you'll note that fine white root tendrils have spread from the original potting soil to draw sustenance from the natural soil around it, even in stony soil where a plant without potting soil wouldn't grow. The richest potting soil is sure to be depleted of nutrients as a plant grows, starving it to death, but outdoor growers in many places can get away with using no fertilizer at all.

PART TWO

Nuts and Bolts of Growing Your Own Marijuana—

HOW TO SPROUT, GROW, TRANSPLANT, AND PROTECT YOUR CROP

CHAPTER 4

Sprouting Seeds

Step Four: Life for all seed-based plants begins when a dormant seed is coaxed into activation by "sprouting" small leaves and a root stem. To truly begin your growing project, you must decide how you want to sprout and how to protect your young plants.

Focus Points:
- **Sprouting Marijuana Seeds: Indoor and Outdoor Methods**
- **Healthy Sprouts: What to Look For**
- **How to Protect Young Plants**

You have your supplies. You've read the basic background information. You know what to expect as your project evolves and as your plant grows. Welcome to the new age—you're now ready to start growing your own marijuana plants.

Growing your own weed can be a fulfilling and incredibly relaxing personal experience. There's a lot to know, but, remember, you're ultimately cultivating a living thing. You don't need to have a master's degree in science to get a great crop. You just need to be attentive to your plant. Be aware of what it needs as it passes through different stages of growth. Pay attention to potential threats (natural and otherwise) from both indoor and outdoor environments. Ultimately, follow your own common sense.

Sprouting Marijuana Seeds: Indoor and Outdoor Methods

The first step for growing your own plants is to sprout the seeds. This "sprouting" process is the moment when you coax a dormant seed into beginning the growth cycle. Whether you are planning to be an indoor grower or an outdoor grower, sprouting is a great pastime that someone once described as a shorter, less troublesome way to indulge parental instincts. It has tangible rewards for success and few repercussions for failure.

A cannabis seed sprouted from a peat pot.

Peat plugs are a good way to turn seeds into sprouts.

Numerous methods are used to sprout seeds. Depending on your resources and spatial capacity, you will want to weigh the pros and cons to decide if you're going to sprout your plants indoors or outside.

Indoor Sprouting—Closet System

If possible—and especially if you live at a latitude where long winters keep growing seasons short—I recommend getting a jump on nature by sprouting seeds inside. (By starting the seedlings that are featured throughout this book in a controlled environment, a month before the snow had melted, I gave my plants a valuable leg up in terms of survival. When the weather grew warm enough to support them outside, my sprouts had already become plants with two or more tiers of leaves, and had a much better chance of surviving the hazards of outdoor growing.)

Sprouting in a closet can be a simple operation that is inexpensive, easy, and successful. The surest method is always one that closely emulates the way a seed sprouts in nature, while providing an ideal environment in which a seed can take root and grow strong with minimal stress or hardship. Begin with a good starting soil, just as you would when growing outside, or use a tray of peat starter plugs, like those that started the crop grown to illustrate this book.

Proper lighting is critical for sprouting, and it doesn't need to be sophisticated, either. A simple grow lamp, available for under $10 at a hardware store, is sufficient to start a dozen seedlings in a peat tray or 2-gallon pot (see **Chapter Five** for more information on indoor equipment and specific lighting needs). Keep the room (and the soil) in which seeds are being sprouted at **70° F or warmer**, and keep the **light burning twenty-four hours a day** until the seeds begin to sprout. After sprouts take root and stand upright, you can cut the light's on-time to twenty hours.

Some inexpensive grow lamps aren't bright enough to satisfy the needs of fledgling cannabis plants, which will show if that's a problem by stretching away on long whitish stems, reaching for more sunlight. The solution is to provide more light; you can add additional grow lamps, surround the stems out to their pot's edges with reflective foil-laminated mylar (the inside of potato chip bags)—which also helps to slow evaporation

Peat plugs planted with seeds ready to sprout.

Seeds beginning to sprout identify themselves with split hulls that exude tiny white tails that will drive themselves into the soil to become roots.

of soil moisture—or place inexpensive full-length mirrors (under $15 at department stores) on the sides to amplify light.

Or you can use an old-fashioned sprouting technique that has worked for generations of tomato growers, and simply sprout your seeds on a sunlit windowsill. Wherever you are on earth, the sun moves across the sky from east to west, but if you're anywhere north of the equator, the sun makes that daily transit across the southern sky. Sprouting seeds and young plants placed in a south-facing window in Montana are in place to receive sunlight from dawn till sunset.

Indoor Sprouting—Napkin Method

Some growers like to start their seeds by keeping them covered in the folds of a paper napkin that lies in a saucer of clean water to which two or three drops of Miracle-Gro liquid houseplant food has been added. Seeds are kept in a sunny location to enhance their motivation to sprout and checked once daily to ensure that they are being kept moist and that no mold has begun around the seed hulls. Seeds that germinate identify

A newly sprouted seedling; note the seed hull still hanging from the sprout's sucker leaves.

themselves by growing a "tail" of whitish root from their split hulls; these should be placed immediately in a tray of saturated peat plugs, which are kept moist at all times from then onward (see **Chapter Two** section "Soils That Work" for more information on peat plugs).

Outdoor Sprouting—Sowing Seeds in Soil

The natural and most commonly used method of sowing marijuana seeds outdoors is to simply scatter them atop a patch of well broken-up ("fluffy") topsoil that has been saturated with a water/fertilizer mix. If you live in a populated area where tap water comes from a municipal water treatment plant, you might consider obtaining water for your crop from a nearby well, stream, or lake. Chlorinated and fluoridated water doesn't seem to grow plants as well as natural, mineral-rich water. (I wonder if that might not also explain why so many people are willing to pay for a bottle of drinking water these days.)

Sprouting is a time when attrition rates are high, especially for outdoor growers who must contend with squirrels and mice that find marijuana shoots delectable, with garden slugs that can wipe out a fledgling crop overnight, and with the whims of changing seasons. It pays to sow at least ten seeds for every plant you expect to harvest in autumn. Even those that make it far enough to sprout their first pair of single-lobed spear-shaped leaves may experience another 30 percent die-off—I once had a coyote pee on a half dozen thriving plants, killing them as effectively as weed poison.

Excess marijuana can be stored for at least five years in a dry place without losing potency, and probably most growers wouldn't view having more harvest than they'd expected as a negative, so I say plant all the seeds you've brought in small, well-separated, preprepared (potting soil mix and fertilizer) plots that receive a maximum of sunlight. When the plants begin to sprout, water them daily— outdoor growers cannot usually overwater their plants—and when plots become crowded with thriving young plants, transplant the largest and strongest of them to other preprepared plots (that process is explained in detail further on).

Sprouting need not be a complex operation; this cardboard egg crate whose cups are filled with moist potting soil provides sprouts that are easy to transplant.

Healthy Sprouts: What to Look For

Once you've decided how you want to sprout, you want to know what to look for to make sure your seeds have been activated. A seed that sprouts will split along the seam that joins the halves of its husk, and within just a few hours a whitish tail will appear. Driven by gravity or instinct, the tail grows longer rapidly, screwing its way down into the soil until the fledgling root can supply sufficient leverage to raise the husk containing the two seed halves upright. From that position, the two seed halves fold out to act as biological solar panels that gather energy and begin a plant's first chlorophyll production even as the tiny taproot sprouts hairlike feeder roots that stretch outward to strengthen its grip on the earth.

From the center of where the seed halves split, the first "sucker" leaves will begin to emerge as soon as they are exposed enough to do so. Cannabis sucker leaves resemble spearmint leaves, being spearhead-shaped with no lobes, heavily veined, and fuzzed over with fine hairs that give them a rough texture. From the center of the pair of sucker leaves, the first pair of lobed leaves will grow from either side of a lengthening stalk; these will almost always be three-lobed "chicken-foot" leaves. If your plant grows successfully, the next pair of leaves will be five-lobed, then seven-lobed. A healthy sprouting state can lead to an excellent vegetative period. It is not unheard of for former seedlings reach about 4 feet tall in late July, growing an inch higher each day, and sprouting a new pair of hand-length uppermost "sun" leaves about every two days.

How to Protect Young Plants

Young plants will of course be kept from view, even where growing cannabis is legal, but also give thought to placing starter pots in protected locations (atop a roof is ideal if it's feasible), and preferably under a ventilated clear plastic bubble. Transparent shields that help to thwart insects and rodents bent on eating your sprouts can be made by cutting plastic soda or water bottles in half, punching small ventilation slots around the perimeter of the lower half, then covering your plant with the inverted

cup. Cannabis shoots have proved to be remarkably tough against cold, and there have been numerous times when I've brought snow-covered trays of tiny seedlings into the house, where they showed themselves to be unharmed by the experience. Even so, very cold nights—20°F or below—can freeze a sprout solid, killing it, so it pays to have a few of these inexpensive pop-bottle shields on hand in early spring.

Next to keeping your seedlings constantly moist, the most important element a cannabis sprout needs is sunlight, as much as it can get. In northern latitudes where

Commercial peat-plug trays with new sprouts.

spring days are short, a problem that outdoor growers contend with is sprouts with green sucker leaves reaching desperately for sunlight at the end of a stem that keeps growing until it cannot support itself. More sophisticated growers sprout their seeds in an indoor grow closet, where young plants are bombarded with enough light and heat to make their first leaves large and lush, at the end of a short, stout stem, and ready for transplanting as soon as the snow melts. Outdoors-only growers must nurture those long, delicate stems by propping them up with sticks or wires to keep the stem from rotting against earth that must be kept wet, and to force tiny sucker leaves to face the sun they vitally need to grow more leaves and a stronger stem. With a little TLC, most long-stemmed shoots can survive to become 5-foot plants.

How Much Light Do Plants Require? This is a question you will be asking yourself both as a grower and as an environmental designer. Your plants' needs will change based on where they are in their life cycle and what type of environment you ultimately decide to grow them in.

Sufficient light is especially critical at the delicate sprouting stage, when you almost can't give seedlings too much light. The most obvious

sign that growing cannabis plants—especially newly sprouted seedlings—aren't getting adequate light is an elongation of whitish stems and stalks caused by leaves reaching desperately upward in search of light. If they don't get it, branches will become so long that they can't

The long stems on these new shoots are caused by sucker leaves reaching upward for more light—they need more light intensity.

support themselves and fall down, sometimes breaking, but frequently developing a potentially fatal rot wherever a stem lies against damp earth. The crop grown for this book was sprouted in a porch window a month before winter's snow had melted. Weak northern spring sunlight made it necessary to actually prop seedling stems above the ground with small Y-shaped twigs until they grew enough leaf area to absorb enough light to nourish a strong growth structure.

Generally speaking, the more light the better where plants are concerned, but there is a point at which plants can no longer assimilate all of the light that shines on them. This is called the light saturation point, and for a typical adult plant it is around about 500 µmol/m². For contrast, the PAR available on a bright summer day is about 2000 µmol/m². Subjecting plants to light beyond their particular saturation point is wasteful of light and usually of electricity, and is actually counterproductive because plant growth slows in too-bright light—like lazy couch potatoes, they stop reaching for the sun because it isn't necessary.

The simplest way to regulate the light particle density radiated onto your plants is only as complicated as raising the grow lamps to lessen light intensity or lowering them to increase it. A standard 130-watt LED grow light can deliver between 200–1400 µmol/m² as its height is varied from 3 feet to 6 inches.

It's important to note that plants don't use both ends of the spectrum adjacent to the green portion at the same time. Blue light is needed mostly during the leafy summer stage and the red spectrum during blooming.

CHAPTER 5

Transplanting

Step Five: **Once your plants have established a stable root system, they are ready for a period of major foliage growth. It's time to set up your permanent growing system. To accomplish this, you will need to learn how to safely transplant your young crop and to decide where you can permanently house your plants.**

Congratulations! You're now the proud parent of several dozen sprouting seeds. But you're far from done. Since you're probably not reading this while wearing the same pair of shoes you picked out when you were ten, you're most likely familiar with the concept of outgrowing stuff.

No matter what system you used to sprout your seeds, you are eventually going to need to move the plants from their original container to a more permanent environment. The process of moving your plants from one container to another is a serious step in plant growth. If the transplant is done poorly, the plant can suffer from shock—leaves will turn yellow, wither, and eventually

Focus Points:
- **Transplanting: When and How to Transplant**
- **Requirements for Thriving Plants**
- **Indoor Growing Systems**
- **Brief Overview of Hydroponic Systems**
- **Security and Other Major Concerns**
- **A Final Word of Caution: Your Safety**

die. If the trauma is too severe, the whole plant will eventually succumb. If done correctly, transplanting can allow your plant to reach maturity rapidly and with minimal support and care.

Now is also the time to decide how you want to set up your permanent growing environment. Some growers choose to keep their entire crop indoors, their plants growing in large individual containers. This situation allows for much more environmental control but also demands more resources and energy to be expended by the grower. Everything from light to food and water must be provided by human engineering. Other growers choose to plant their marijuana directly in the earth. This can lead to a much less costly experience in terms of time and energy. But picking a permanent outdoor site raises several major issues for any grower. Not only does the location have to meet certain horticultural standards, but crop security, personal safety, and overall accessibility all have to be considered.

After reading this chapter, you will know not only *how* to move your crop but also *where* you want to move it to permanently.

Transplanting: When and How to Transplant

Cannabis plants seem to have a mind of their own, and whatever container you start yours in, they will rapidly expand their root systems to reach the walls that contain them. (Oddly, because plants in open ground seem less anxious about their freedom, and seldom develop root balls greater than 18 inches in diameter; but let a plant mature in a 55-gallon drum, and its roots will reach to its walls.) If a plant becomes root-bound, as marijuana

This female cannabis plant grew too large for its pot and was transplanted at four months; it yielded 2 ounces of bud.

plants are likely to do in any container whose capacity is under 4 gallons, it just stops growing.

The same problem is seen with peat plugs; just when a plant begins to take off for its spring growing spurt, its roots become bound by the fine mesh that covers and holds peat plugs in shape. In a perfect world all plant roots can easily grow through this delicate netting, but in the real world most marijuana plants will become trapped and root-bound, and will cease to grow.

When to Transplant

As your marijuana plants thrive they will begin to move from the "sprouting" stage into the "seedling" stage. Marijuana plants are still quite small during this "seedling" stage. After sprouting your seeds, you will see two oblong leaves ("cotyledons") emerge from the small stem that has risen from the dirt. Within a few days these two odd leaves will give way to "true leaves" that are visibly recognizable as marijuana leaves. This stage is critical for root growth, and while you may not see a lot going on above the dirt, your

Transplanted into a plain coffee container at one month. This two-month-old cannabis plant can be transplanted into open ground any time.

plants will be busy establishing a fragile but essential root system in whatever sprouting medium you chose.

Your plants are too young to move during the "seedling" stage, but as with the "sprouting" stage, you need to make sure your plants are provided with light and constantly moist dirt. This stage of life will usually last anywhere from two to six weeks.

You will know your plant is ready to move by the sudden increase in rapid leaf growth. More and more "true leaves" will begin appearing, and the stem will be firm enough for you to grasp gently without damaging the plant. Once you start to notice

"Vegetative" growth is hugely exciting for any grower. It is the rapid-fire period when your plants really begin to take off and thrive. A healthy plant in the vegetative stage will exhibit massive increases in foliage production. Vertical growth can even be as fast as 1 to 2 inches a day. A plant in vegetative state is when you really begin to see your efforts paying off.

However, none of this is possible if your plant has stunted roots or not enough room to grow. That is why it is **critical to transplant your marijuana seedlings when the plant is just on the cusp of the vegetative state.** If you move your plant too soon, it will not be strong enough to survive the shock caused by a change in its environment. If you wait too long, you risk retarding your plant's growth—possibly even permanently. (For more information on the stages of growth, see "Marijuana Life Cycle" at the beginning of this book.)

Large transplant pots can be used to grow—or sprout—seedlings until they reach transplantable size.

these changes, your plant is officially moving from the "seedling" stage to the "vegetative" growth phase.

Peat plugs are a great way to start your crop earlier when you live where growing seasons are short, but be prepared to transplant seedlings to a larger pot or to the outside as soon as you can see white root tendrils emerging beneath the mesh, or you might stunt the plant's growth permanently.

How to Transplant

Any grower has three basic options when replanting vegetative-stage marijuana. First, you can decide to continue growing your plant indoors in an easily accessible but discreet location. Second, you can pick a location in the great outdoors where you can monitor your crop while taking advantage of natural resources like water and sunlight. Third, you can decide to move your plant into a larger container (a 55-gallon barrel, for example) and then move that container to a temporary outdoor location. This third option allows for rapid crop relocation to avoid hazards such as law enforcement detection or the unexpected appearance of local pests.

There are definite advantages and disadvantages to all three situations. But for the most part, the actual process of moving your plant(s) from one container to another is fairly straightforward.

Young plants transplanted into open soil at two months of age.

Whether you're moving a plant directly into the ground, or you're popping your weed in a larger potting vessel (this book recommends an absolute minimum container size of 4 gallons per plant), the first step is to prepare new soil to receive your plants. If you're working in the ground, dig a hole several inches larger than the pot from which a transplant will be taken, but leave excavated soil piled around the outside of the hole, where it can be pushed back in place after transplanting. It is important to transplant plants with the soil in which they have been growing; this helps to eliminate shock that might occur from a sudden change in habitat (closet-grown plants seem especially prone to shock), and eases a plant's transition from potting soil to natural dirt.

Make sure that soil in the pot being transplanted is moist; not so wet that it becomes mud, and not so dry that it crumbles, but moist enough to be firm and to stick together in the shape of its container. Next, place your hand palm-down over the soil in the original container (so that the stalk is between your middle fingers). Place your other palm under the pot's bottom, and in one smooth motion turn the pot upside down, emptying its contents into the hand around the stalk. Put down the discarded container and place your free hand under the plant's bottom (white root tendrils should be visible) and gently lower the roots into the hole you've dug for them.

If chunks of dirt break off from the root ball, don't worry; just get the roots immediately into the ground and re-covered with soil. Surrounded by good soil instead of water, there is no more need to hold a peat plug together, so the mesh surrounding them should be torn free entirely and thrown away. Saturate the soil all around the plant with a gallon of water enriched with the prescribed amount of plant food. Finally, cover over exposed soil around the transplant with leaves and ground debris from the surrounding area, not only to make the plant less noticeable but also to inhibit the evaporation of water from below.

Where to Move: Requirements for Thriving Plants

If you create a hospitable zone for it, virtually any living thing can live surrounded by the most inhospitable environment, a theory that has already been demonstrated on a grand scale by orbiting space stations and undersea habitats. It follows that marijuana plants can also be induced to thrive outside almost anywhere that has a growing season.

Watch the Sun, Look for the Water

When selecting a transplant location, consider how well it provides for the needs of your plants. Only at the equator is the sun directly overhead, so any latitude north of that places the sun in the southern sky; an ideal transplant site would be a low, bald south-facing ridge that is open to the east and west and bathed in sunlight from dawn to dusk.

Water is an important consideration. I have been lucky enough to grow on rich swampland knolls where a hole dug more than a foot struck water, and plants more than a foot tall needed no watering for the entire summer. Streambanks, lake and pond shore-lines, and dry marshes can be great transplant locations, although it might be necessary to clear an opening to the sky from cattails and other underbrush. One problem with open wetlands is that most ponds, lakeshores, and riverbanks are favored by wandering anglers and explorers; not everyone can recognize cannabis growing in a natural environment, but few who do will leave your crop unmolested.

Almost as though it realizes that its roots are no longer constrained, this young cannabis transplant is growing fast.

Just ten weeks old, this young marijuana plant is strong and vivacious.

Another problem with growing in constantly moist soil is that it frequently doesn't provide the solid footing that a growing marijuana plant needs for its roots to get a solid grip.

Planters vs. Directly Growing in the Ground

Plants growing free in the earth seem to always achieve more size, with greater health, and lusher foliage, probably because no environment is more natural than nature, not even where short growing seasons don't allow time for maximum growth. One downside is that plants outside are subject to a range of dangers not encountered by closet growers. Seldom will indoor growers see the tiny red spider mites that enweb and kill the leaves of outdoor plants, but there are other dangers, which will be addressed further

Even in a 5-gallon bucket, this pair of adult cannabis plants have become root-bound; one must be removed (transplanted) to give the other room to grow.

on (for more information regarding specific threats from outdoor pests, see the section in chapter 7 entitled "Outdoor Dangers: Common Pests and Problems").

If your growing pots are large enough, there is no need to transplant. As long as a location provides maximum sunlight, plants are watered—sometimes up to a gallon per plant per day if the harvest angels smile on you—and plants are not eaten by animals and insects, a potted plant with at least a foot of growing room for its roots in all directions can be grown to fruition. Favored, and ideal, outside growing vessels are the 5- and 6-gallon plastic buckets that are used ubiquitously for everything from drywall mud and restaurant pickles to carry-kit/seat combos that have become popular with deer hunters. Relatively easy to carry by their wire-bail handles, even when weighted with moist dirt, these buckets, and similar-size pots, provide ample water storage for the hottest and driest places, with enough root space to satisfy the largest hemp plant. An added advantage is that some of the most willing pot-plant-eaters are unable to climb the smooth sides of a plastic bucket. A downside is that many buckets are brightly colored and must be spray-painted, draped with camouflage mosquito netting, partially buried, or otherwise covered with debris and materials that make them hard to notice.

Where to Move: Indoor Growing Systems

For some growers in some places, it might not be feasible to grow plants outside; even in a world where cannabis is legalized across the board, there are sure to be social derelicts who find it preferable to steal the fruits of someone else's labors than to grow their own. It has already happened, with at least one fatal but (oddly) legally justifiable shooting in California. Produce farmers have always contended with human marauders, and it seems likely that marijuana buds would attract far more dangerous predators than carrots or cabbage ever did.

Marijuana grow rooms range from small closets to large pole barns.

The answer is to grow your plants under artificial or hybrid artificial/natural conditions where they're protected from harsh or abrupt weather changes, a habitat where every facet of plant life can be rigidly controlled at every stage to assure the most ideal environment. Hybrid growing operations provide plants with both natural and artificial elements—greenhouses are an example—while "closet" systems are nearly or entirely shut off from the outside world.

A hybrid system can be as complex as a heated Lexan greenhouse, or as simple as a few pots set in front of a south-facing (if you're north of the equator) window where plants can absorb sunshine from sunrise to sunset. Some growers believe that natural sunlight, even through glass, is best for plants. A studio apartment with large windows that reach to the floor can be great; it helps to keep plants as low to the floor as possible, because heavier carbon dioxide exhaled by residents—also pets, even pests and vermin—seeks the lowest level, nourishing the plants.

Closed Systems

While window-seat and greenhouse growing operations that use natural sunlight are probably most preferred, many indoor growers also face the problem of having their crops exposed to the world through glass or Plexiglas panes. Where that is a problem, it becomes necessary to create a wholly artificial growing environment in which all of the elements needed to coax maximum growth and THC content from plants is provided by the grower.

Fully enclosed systems are preferred by many very good growers, including legally sanctioned professional commercial operations, because they have potential for being exploited into an environment that enhances, even mutates plants. Intentionally mutated plants grown in closed systems have become the numerous and often outlandish-looking different strains that are available from commercial seed firms. I have to admit that the potency of some indoor-grown buds is very good, because savvy growers can not only manipulate the nutrition administered to produce the botanical equivalent of a steroid-enhanced athlete but also extend the growing season beyond anything found on earth. They can vary the "days," the durations of light and darkness, to any desired combination—like twenty-five hours of light followed by six hours of darkness for a period of twelve months.

When deciding how to set up your permanent growing system, weigh the plants' needs against your own capacity. Do you have the room to grow inside? Are you willing to foot the electric bill?

Grow Room Operation

Operating a grow room is easier than growing outdoors because everything you need is in one conveniently accessed location. Follow the same soil, fertilizer, and watering instructions given in the beginning chapters of this book, give growing plants plenty of bright light from sprout to maturity, and pluck your leaves to stimulate production of THC.

Typical duration of light and darkness for growing plants is twenty hours of bright light at an ambient temperature of about 70°F, followed by four hours of "sleep" time, during which plants continue to grow while resting. When plants reach the desired height, cut back the daylight and dark hours to twelve and twelve (some growers alternate times beyond normal twenty-four-hour cycles) to fool them into believing that the shortened days of autumn have come. Fewer hours of light induces plants to flower, bud, and pollinate in preparation for what they perceive as the onset of winter.

Grow Lights

Plants photosynthesize carbon dioxide into the organic material that makes up the plant (carbon, proteins, sugars . . .) using solar energy derived from sunlight. That energy is absorbed through specialized proteins with chlorophyll molecules that are contained in photosynthetic cell membranes called chloroplasts. Chlorophyll absorbs mostly reds and blues, but this green-colored plant blood is poor at absorbing light from the green part of the spectrum, because those wavelengths are reflected away. Chlorophyll absorbs so much red and blue light at either end of the green wavelengths that no colors except green are visible in most foliage until autumn, when the chlorophyll decays and other colors are revealed.

There are two types of chlorophyll: Chlorophyll a and Chlorophyll b (note the lower-case designator). These differ slightly in chemical composition and frequencies of light absorbed. Type a absorbs violet and red portions of the spectrum at 430 to 662 nanometers (nm); Type b absorbs blue through yellow, at 453 to 642 nm. Together the chlorophylls absorb what is called Photosynthetically Available Radiation (PAR), defined as a spectral band between 400 (purple) and 700 (red) nanometers that a majority of leafing plants find necessary for photosynthesis. The unit of measure for PAR is derived from the number of light particles, or micromoles (μmol), per square meter per second that strike a surface. This value provides a logarithmic Photosynthetic Photon Flux Density (PPFD) index number that can be used to determine how much usable light is being radiated onto your plants.

LED lights are the latest in cool-burning, efficient grow room lighting technology

LED Grow Lights

Light emitting diodes (LEDs) have revolutionized the lighting world in recent years. LEDs are low voltage, with long battery life for flashlights. They produce as much or more brightness than incandescent bulbs, and they emit very little heat—in fact, it might be necessary to heat your grow room. But it won't be necessary to have cooling fans and ducts, and it won't be quite so critical to have a fire extinguisher mounted nearby. An added bonus might be that the low heat output of LED arrays makes them almost undetectable to thermal imaging devices that can easily spot the infrared emitted by conventional high-pressure sodium grow lights. Incandescent grow lights can also be noisier than a discreet grower might like; high-pressure sodium units definitely emit a power hum that can be heard in another room, especially at start-up.

Be aware that not all LEDs are the same: Check the power rating (wattage) and stated luminous flux (lumens)—in general, the higher the value of either, the brighter the light. Also look for quality-brand LEDs, like Cree Procyon or Philips Luxeon. When shopping for an LED grow light, be sure to limit your choices to purpose-built models with LEDs that are "tuned" to emit increased light at the four color peaks most needed by plants.

LED grow lights aren't less expensive than conventional grow lights and usually cost more than incandescent systems. The initial outlay of cash causes many growers to balk at converting their grow rooms to LED, but the payback is immediate and rewarding. Up to 90 percent of the electricity required to light filament-type bulbs is wasted as heat, so it follows that cooler LED lights can produce the same number of lumens at considerably lower wattage. Experts estimate that an average grower can pay off his or her investment in electrical savings in one to two years.

If saving energy and reducing the possibility of setting your home on fire aren't convincing enough, LED lights require virtually no maintenance or replacement—now that's a quality I especially admire in a piece of equipment. Some manufacturers claim 100,000 hours of life from their LEDs, which equates to more than ten years of use.

Fluorescent Lights

Another alternative to conventional high-pressure sodium and metal halide grow lights is a compact fluorescent fixture, like those sold in department stores for use as under-the-cupboard counter lights. Retail is about ten bucks for these basically disposable fixtures (you can replace the compact tubes, if you can find them), making them especially attractive to first-timers and to growers who must operate on a shoe-string. Some growers report good results from using the spiral-type fluorescents that screw into conventional light sockets, claiming that these can be more easily moved around as needed to help maximize growth.

Fluorescents aren't as bright as incandescent bulbs or LEDs, but they do produce most of the light a plant needs to grow, and they run much cooler than filament bulbs, so they can be placed within inches of a plant without burning the foliage. One grower uses a combination of fluorescents placed on the floor, shining upward, with more mounted to the walls, and high-pressure sodium lamps above; his results have never been disappointing.

Like LED units, fluorescent grow lamps use a fraction of the electricity needed by lamps that use heated filaments to produce light, which provides the added benefit of reducing electric costs that might be monitored by some agencies. They are also less obvious as a heat source to infrared detectors.

Reflectors

Reflective surfaces can effectively increase the intensity of any light, and they're a must-have for any closed growing system. My favorite setup was one of cheap (about $5 each) 1 x 4-foot department store mirrors stood against the walls. Additional mirrors on the floor reflected light back upward, against the underside of leaves that never receive direct sunlight in nature. One drawback was that the mirrors had to be wiped (not sprayed directly with a cleaner that could mist onto your plants) regularly to keep them reflecting at maximum intensity.

A poor person's alternative to mirrors is to simply line the walls and floor with aluminum foil, taped or push-pinned as needed to hold it in desired locations. The shiny side of food-wrap foil is highly reflective, as well as inexpensive. It's impractical to clean

because of its innate flimsiness, but is easy and cheap to replace as necessary. I've also used squares of foil with narrow slots cut from one edge to their centers as underside-reflectors. Sliding the foil's slot around a plant's stalk to its center throws light back upward from below to help maximize growth, and the foil acts as a vapor shield, holding back moisture that would otherwise evaporate from the soil.

Finally, there's the really cheap, yet effective, potato-chip-bag reflector. Chips are often sold in Mylar bags that are not by themselves an adequate moisture barrier, and so are layered on the inside with a fine coat of reflective foil. Walls of taped-together chip bags are a cheapskate's delight, but be aware that they melt easily and burn freely once ignited.

Carbon-Dioxide Generators

Plants breathe carbon dioxide, so it makes sense to grow them in an environment that provides as much of that necessary gas as possible. Plants that I've grown in an enclosed CO_2-rich atmosphere have demonstrated remarkably accelerated growth—you can see the effect right away—kind of like accelerating healing in medical patients by feeding pure oxygen into their lungs.

Try to locate your growing room next to a gas appliance whenever possible to take advantage of carbon dioxide created by combustion in gas hot water heaters and furnaces. Pot-growing experts generally agree that 70°F is about ideal for growing cannabis, and gas-burning appliances help to keep plants warm on cold nights, while traces of heavier CO_2 that escapes being exhausted with more dangerous gases can be used to help your plants grow faster.

Probably the best CO_2 generator is a simple low-pressure tank that would ordinarily be used to put carbonation into soft drinks, pressurize beer kegs, or power paintball guns. They range in volume from 20 ounces to more than 20 pounds, with prices ranging from about $25 for the former to about $100 for the latter. Some growers like to slowly bleed their tanks from a hose or hoses suspended directly over their plants, keeping them constantly refreshed with a flow of pure CO_2. Others prefer to semiseal their grow room entrances with a plastic shower curtain and flood the growing space with carbon dioxide for about twenty seconds (presuming a small space of 4x6 feet or so) before sealing it for the next couple of hours. This hyperbaric chamber for plants really helps to accelerate growth and at the same time makes your plants unpleasant places for spider mites and other oxygen-breathing pests.

CO_2 can also be generated by chemical processes. One of the simplest is to burn a safely enclosed (glass-jarred) candle inside your sealed grow room. So long as the candle is burning, it produces carbon dioxide, and little else, as the result of combustion. If the candle goes out before being consumed (unlikely), the atmosphere inside is saturated with carbon dioxide.

Another simple CO_2 generator is a bottle of ordinary vinegar that has been suspended (duct-taped) upside down at a height of about one foot over a bowl filled with plain baking soda. A small (wire brad-size) hole in the center of the vinegar bottle's cap permits—ideally—about one drop a minute to fall into the soda below, where acid and caustic react mildly to produce carbon dioxide gas.

Where to Move: Brief Overview of Hydroponic Systems

As you consider what type of permanent growing system to set up, you're going hear a lot of talk about hydro-systems and hydroponics. The term "hydroponic" literally translates as "water work" and refers to a specific method of metabolism where a plant absorbs all nutrients through a soil-less medium. This doesn't necessarily mean all hydroponic plants grow in a glass of water. In the last 20 years, advances in hydro-technology have allowed growers to create growing beds out of everything from plastic baskets to blocks of rockwool insulation. (Technically, the peat plugs described in "Chapter Two: Soil" are actually soil-less and therefore hydroponic).

In order to thrive, a marijuana plant only needs: water, light, oxygen, nutrients, and carbon-dioxide. Plopping a seed down in a plot of dirt is the "tried and true" way to meet these demands, but that doesn't mean it's necessarily the most efficient method. The main principle behind hydroponic farming is the idea that a plant which does not have to expend energy searching for nutrients in soil will instead allocate those resources to fruit and leaf production. Rather than rely on fertilizers to ensure plants have the nutrients they need to thrive in a plot of soil, hydroponic farmers create "nutrient solutions" which are directly applied to the root system itself.

DWC systems are basic but effective. The key is to make sure the stagnant solution is aerated enough to allow direct nutrient absorption by the roots.

Because marijuana plants can use nutrients as soon as they are absorbed, *cannabis* often grows extremely fast in soil-less gardens. That being said, hydroponic systems require a high level of research, maintenance, and overall investment. They can also be more unforgiving of mistakes made while trying to learn how to manage your system.

Personally, I have found that the best way to be a single, self-sufficient grower, is to go back to basics – pick up your seeds and get ready to get your hands dirty. However, no "how to grow" manual would be complete without a section on hydroponics. Below is a brief overview of the several methods for hydroponic growth. Before you decide to set up a soilless system, research your local vendors to make sure you have the resources and space necessary to set up a hydro-system.

Five Soilless Systems

Generally, hydroponic systems actually use less water than soil-based systems. However, if you're setting up a hydro-system you're going to have to encounter all the costs that come with setting up an indoor growing environment (see: **Indoor Growing Systems**). In addition, you may find yourself spending more money on fertilizers and growing mediums (see: *Vermiculite and Perlite* in **Chapter Three: Fertilizers**). Nutrient solution mixtures will be an additional, but completely justified cost, as well. Luckily, hobby hydroponics has taken off in the past ten years and numerous online vendors can offer competitive prices for everything from supplies to complete soilless systems. However, before you spend any cash, you'll want to have a basic hydroponic vocabulary so you can shop intelligently.

- **Deep Water Culture (DWC)**

   This is one of the easiest systems to build and maintain. The investment is minimal, and the general rule of thumb is one unit per plant. In its most basic form a DWC consists of three parts. The first piece is a light-sealed reservoir where the nutrient solution is stored (protection from light ensures algae and other impurities won't be able to grow and pollute the solution). The second section is usually a small bucket or net filled with a growing medium (rockwool, perlite etc.) which hangs above the nutrient solution. *Think of a 5 gallon bucket with a perlit-filled basket suspended from a hole in lid.* It's vital that the second piece be made of a mesh or porous material so that the roots can grow down towards the nutrient solution without being hemmed in. The final piece of the DWC setup is an "airstone" placed within the nutrient solution itself. "Airstones" can be found in any pet supply store near the aquarium section. Used in fish tanks, airstones naturally release oxygen into any water based solution.

   DWC systems are hydroponics at its most basic. The advantage is a rich and easily accessible supply of nutrients for your plants. But dangers arise whenever a water source remains stagnant. Keep an eye out for root rot or parasites which can thrive in nutrient rich water. Make sure each container is light-sealed to prevent algae growth.

- **Top Feed**

   Similar to the DWC, top feed hydro-systems are fairly simple to set up and easy to maintain. As with DWC, a reservoir of nutrient solution is placed below a porous container holding a plant. The plant should be growing in a soilless medium and a hose should be placed at the base of the stalk. This hose is connected via a pump to the nutrient solution. Several times a day, a timer activates the pump and the solution is rained down over the root system. At the same time, anything not absorbed is collected as it drains from the porous and soilless medium back into the resevoir. *Think of it as a fountain for your pot plant.* The advantage to top feeders is that they are easy to maintain and reliable. You have the option of setting up one unit per plant, or buying pots big enough to house several small plants at once. However, your initial investment is going to be a bit more than if you were working with a simple DWC system and if your pump breaks, you have to react fairly quickly to make sure the roots don't dry out and die.

- **Ebb and Flow/Flood and Drain**

  The name says it all, ebb and flow systems involve soaking plant roots in a nutrient solution for a set amount of time, draining the roots, and then repeating the process several times a day. Most systems involve a water-tight table or plant bed which holds several large plants growing out of

Ebb and flow provides a great way to grow several small plants at once.

blocks rockwool (or some other soilless medium). Much like the top-feeding system, ebb and flow offers the advantage of not dealing with stagnant water (which can lead to root rot, parasite infestations etc.) The disadvantages come from increased investment and multiple plant exposure. Ebb and flow systems are built to accommodate more than one plant at a time. If your solution needs tweaking, or a parasite has entered the water, you're going to lose multiple units rather than just one plant.

- **Nutrient Film/Flow Technique (NFT)**

  Effective, but equipment reliant, NFT hydroponic systems use capillary mats as the medium which connects roots to the nutrient solution. Most NFT

plants are sprouted normally, but the seedlings are then suspended so that the roots enter a growing chamber which exists as a layer between the solution reservoir and the spouted plants. The bottom

Constant access to a nutrient rich solution lets these lettuce plants thrive in a hydroponic setup.

of the growing chamber is lined with capillary mats which are then covered in a constant flow of nutrient solution from a pump connected to the reservoir below. These mats are key to this system, and a great growing tool to keep around even if you're growing non-hydroponically. Capillary mats are made of an extremely porous material which absorbs water rapidly but dispels liquid at a much slower and more constant rate. The advantage to the NFT system is that is regulates the roots' exposure to liquid (preventing drowning) but still allows for 24/7 access to the nutrient solution. Unfortunately, with more components to maintain and equipment to buy, the NFT also requires a deeper investment of time and energy on the part of the growers.

- **Aeroponics and Misting**

  Areoponics and misting can result in amazing crop yields, but the results require a lot of time, effort, and expertise. Most aeroponic set-ups are dependent on an environment which maintains close to 100 percent humidity at all times. Plants are sprouted and hung in soilless mediums (baskets with rockwool or expanded clay balls). Then as roots grow they are simply allowed to hang downwards. The nutrient solution is misted directly onto the roots from a spraying system that is set up and timed. The key to this system is that everything below the stalk (i.e. everything that would not normally grow above the soil) hangs into a sealed environment where the nutrient solution sits and where the misting system has direct access to the roots. Misters draw enriched moisture from the reservoir and anything not absorbed by the roots is allowed to circulate in the artificial environment. Problems arise when rapidly growing roots crowd out smaller roots resulting in uneven distribution. In addition, self-sufficient mister system don't come cheap and can break easily. Salt buildup from the nutrient solution can cause problems with nozzles. If something goes wrong you have to open the entire unit, and you risk drying out your plants. In general, areoponics is a great system (both NASA and Disney actually use it to grow food supplies), but it is not necessarily the best for a small grower whose goal is to create a personal supply of pot.

Nutrient Solution

The major challenge in hydroponic farming is deciding how you're going to deliver nutrients to your crop. Luckily, marijuana requirements do not change whether you're growing in soil, sand, or solution. Overall, making a nutrient solution is fairly simple – most hydroponic suppliers sell solutions that are already mixed and only need water (for more specifics on plant nutrition see **Chapter Three: Fertilizer**). However, since you're working directly with root absorption, you are going to need to pay attention to the pH balance of your solution more than if you were working in soil.

Because your marijuana will be growing faster in a hydro-system, the consequences of an imbalanced solution will build up much faster than they would if you were working with soil. Weed likes to grow in slightly acidic mediums. You're going to want to test your water, and then test your mixed solution every day, and especially before you apply it to your crop. Most growers recommend keeping your pH somewhere between 5.5 and 6.8; the ideal lies somewhere in the middle around 6.15. If you find your solution is too acidic or too basic you can easily buy products specifically designed to raise or lower the pH levels of your plant food without causing unwanted side effects.

- **More Research**

Hydroponic growing requires a significant support system and almost constant availability (in case something goes wrong). Before you decide to invest ask yourself several questions to decide if this is the right system for you:

- Do you have the space for a grow room that will require a constant flow of water?
- Are you willing to pay electrical bills for grow lamps, heated water, and equipment (timers, pump etc.)?
- Are there suppliers nearby where you can re-stock if something goes wrong or are you dependant on internet vendors?
- Are you willing to keep track of minute details on a day to day basis (pH balance, water levels, nutrient imbalances etc.)?
- How much research have you done on the specific system you've chosen to work with? Are there sources you can turn to for troubleshooting or if something goes wrong?

In the past most hydroponic growers were commercially based. Elaborate systems were set up and maintained in order to yield large crops that could be harvested and sold for profit. However, in the past ten years hydroponics has become a hobby sport for gardeners who cultivate everything from weed to tomatoes and herbs. Entire kits for individual hydro-growers can be bought at almost any major gardening supply company in the U.S. If you've never grown pot before, soil may be the best way to start learning the ins and outs of marijuana cultivation. If you've already cultivated a few plants and feel confident enough, then hydroponics may be the best next step for your garden.

Security and Other Major Concerns

I cannot stress this concept enough: Silence is Golden. Most important for every grower, legal or outlaw—and this bears repeating as often as necessary, especially to yourself—keep your trap shut about where you're growing your herb. According to police officers themselves, most growing operations that have been busted were exposed by friends of a grower, sometimes by a boastful grower himself. Discounting unfortunate circumstance for a grower and lucky good fortune for authorities, few marijuana growing operations are actually found out and busted by old-fashioned detective work. Even in places where growing cannabis has been legalized, remember that nearly all crops that are found and stolen are taken by acquaintances of the grower who discovered—or more likely, were shown—the plants they absconded with. Save being prideful until after the harvest, because if you really want to impress fellow pot smokers, the best way to do it is with a fat joint or bowl filled with really potent herb.

Security

Security is a constant concern, because even if growing marijuana is made entirely legal, it will always remain a highly stealable commodity—even if grown in your own backyard—and there will always be "reapers" who are willing to reap what you and your hard work have sown. I don't use or advocate the use of fishing line strung with hooks, "punji boards" made from nail-filled planks, or any of the other booby traps that some for-profit growers use to discourage thieves. For me, no amount of marijuana is worth harming someone, no matter how questionable that person's genetics or upbringing may be. Besides, trying to protect your plants using violent, hurtful methods that are guaranteed to bring police officers to the site is a poor strategy to start with. Even worse if your victim happens to be a cop, because then you will be actively hunted by vengeful police officers who stick together better than Crips or Bloods, and you'll remain prosecutable for it until the end of your life.

Rangers at Yellowstone and other parks generally concur that backpackers and hikers rarely venture more than 200 yards off the trail, and being just 300 yards from a trail is almost a guarantee that you won't see another person. My own experiences as both a pot grower and a professional outdoorsman only confirm that assertion. Many

This recently transplanted adult has adapted to its now home without so much as a hiccup.

have been the times when I was hunkered down next to mature 6-foot plants while watching tourists playing with their ATVs on a trail not 100 yards distant.

One advantage outdoor pot growers enjoy is the proof of that old axiom that says at least some people can't see the forest for the trees. The allusion made by this proverb is that a person who finds himself or herself in the midst of an environment unfamiliar to them will often undergo a kind of sensory overload, unable to consciously register all that is present or happening around them. The "busier" or more complex an environment, the less any person's brain is able to take in, and the effect of overstimulation of the visual cortex is amplified when an observer is in unfamiliar surroundings. Outdoor growers can use this phenomenon to their advantage by planting or transplanting in places where other vegetation helps to clutter the visual landscape and make it difficult for the eye to discern specific shapes.

Trails

It is inevitable that any animal or human will fall into regular routines if left unmolested by outside influences for an extended period of time. If those routines take place outside, in a natural environment, any place that is visited regularly is going to be marked with visible trails. No matter how remote or hard to reach your growing site might be, it's a sure bet that you'll naturally select the easiest route to it, and before you know it, your footsteps will have crushed and killed most or all of the vegetation that had been growing on that trail. These ribbons of trampled ground are a flag to any peace officer who sees them, whether a cop or a game warden. Even more likely to follow a path to your crop are mushroom hunters, berry pickers, sport hunters, and day hikers just out exploring the countryside.

For me, the easiest solution to the problem of making trails that might be followed by someone I'd rather not have following them has been to establish several—more than three—routes between a well-traveled trail or road and my hidden crop site. Not many people today are skilled in the ways of tracking, and even the best tracker loses a trail from time to time; your best strategy is to ensure that there is as little sign of your passage as possible. Use existing game trails whenever possible to avoid creating new paths that could be noticed by someone who knows the area intimately. A multitude of trails makes any one of them harder to detect, and harder to cover should your operation attract unwanted attention from authorities, while also increasing the chance that you will notice ambushers in the area before they see you.

Aerial Observation

As country singer Steve Earle noted in his song "Copperhead Road," "The DEA's got a chopper in the air." In fact, scuttlebutt has it that the recent loosening of legal restrictions on marijuana in several states has at the time of this writing prompted federal agencies to withdraw funding for aerial searches to find marijuana plants. If that new policy holds, it's good news for growers because few states have much of an air force, and those in preferred pot-farming regions—like Kentucky and Tennessee—have relied on help from Air National Guard and other federal agencies to find cannabis fields. That would leave individual states to search for cannabis crops using their own funding, and at this time it appears that most states are reassessing what it costs them to track down, prosecute, and imprison otherwise law-abiding citizens for merely possessing a dead plant.

But until—and even if—pot is legalized across the board, personal-use growers should not let their guard down. So long as cannabis is illegal to grow, there's always a chance that some private pilot might fly over at the right altitude, angle, and time to be convinced that there are pot plants there, and then report the coordinates of that observation to authorities. And of course it requires nothing more than a stroke from the right politician's pen to reallocate all of the monies that have been and will be withdrawn from aerial search operations.

Even if cannabis is completely decriminalized and giant agricultural corporations like Cargill are given the nod to grow pot for commercial sale, there are sure to be limitations on how many plants may be grown or how much processed weight can be possessed. The advantage is that you'll be able to grow on your own or borrowed private property (planting on public lands will still be illegal); possible disadvantages

Bottled skunk scent, used by deer hunters to mask their own spoor from game, is a good way to keep exploring humans away from your cannabis crop.

include being prohibited from growing as large a crop as you'd like, and perhaps being forced to purchase a tax stamp. Selling your pot without having necessary licenses and paying applicable taxes will still be a crime, but now it would be tax evasion.

One federal officer I spoke with told me that everyone in his department had been shown training films depicting the methods and equipment used by America's best-trained drug cops, the DEA. One film described how Huey and Black Hawk helicopters, painted black for DEA use, had been outfitted with infrared and ultraviolet spectrographic cameras that could cause light wavelengths unique to cannabis plants to stand out among other foliage. The narrator even went on to claim the equipment was so sensitive that it could identify a single plant among wild foliage.

Fortunately for small growers, cannabis-detection equipment on DEA choppers has proved to be considerably less infallible than training films would have us believe. For this argument I present my own experiences of watching black helicopters flying past low and slow while I tended plants that usually averaged 5 to 6 feet tall. The key to avoiding detection from the air, I believe, is keep the size of what must be exposed to a minimum. More plainly, never grow more than three plants in a single location, and keep plots well separated, with about 50 yards between them in most terrain.

Don't get greedy—as so many do—and grow a crop large enough be seen from space. First, calculate how much bud you'll need to keep yourself comfortably in smoke for twelve months after you harvest—12 ounces, minimum, for me, which is probably about average. Most healthy 4-foot females will produce between 1 and 2 ounces of dried buds (often more, especially where growing seasons are longest). To ensure that you'll have sufficient female plants to provide that amount, estimate that half of your crop will be females.

Smell

I was driving along the US-131 highway in the north woods near Boyne Falls, Michigan, one warm summer evening when the unmistakable spoor of marijuana blew through my open window. It is against my principles to steal another grower's plants (I have been known to pinch a bud as a reward for that integrity, though), but while passing a joint I mentioned the incident to a friend who found five 4-foot plants growing on the far side of a marshy ditch, hidden by willow and dogwood shrubs. The next evening this same unscrupulous person brought the uprooted plants, which had not yet begun to show their gender, to me because he didn't know how to process green weed. I dried and cured it for him, and even smoked some of it—the plants had never been pruned, and their leaves apparently had only small amounts of the insect repellant THC. I wasn't happy about the lack of moral character my smoking buddy had displayed by stealing those fine young plants, and my regret was made more poignant by imagining what they might have become in autumn.

The lesson from this story is that pot plants have a strong, far-reaching scent that anyone who's ever bought a quarter-ounce could recognize from as far off as 200 yards, if the wind was favorable. The plants in my story were in an ideal location, at the side of a busy highway, where probably no one would ever stop their car, jump the wet ditch, and get close enough to differentiate the cannabis plants from the dogwoods, willows, and alders that surrounded their small cleared plot. The grower's downfall lay in not anticipating the pungent, musky aroma given off by fast-growing cannabis plants from midsummer to winter. There's a good chance that many summer motorists with open windows failed to recognize the odor, or mistook the musky smell for that of a skunk (pretty common), but I have found marijuana plants more than a few times just by following my nose.

In most places there are prevailing winds that blow from a predictable direction most of the time—in North America, winds are generally from the southeast in summer. Take prevailing winds, which change direction with the seasons, into consideration when planting or transplanting young plants. Even by the end of July, when plants should be approximately 3 feet tall and growing bushy, there will be a distinctive musky scent that is different from the sweeter aroma of flowering males and females. In this stage of growth, until the males begin to flower in early September, their pungent odor is likely to be recognized only by people who've grown pot and are familiar with the skunky smell of fast-growing summer cannabis. By mid-September, though, everyone who's ever smoked from a Baggie will recognize the almost candylike aroma of maturing buds. Always try to site your growing location where prevailing winds are likely to blow scent from your plants away from populated or even frequented areas. A wilderness location is always preferred if you can get water to your plants, but authorities might be

surprised at how many cannabis crops have been secretly grown and harvested within sight of a busy road, where virtually none of the speeding cars ever stops to look closely at local vegetation. From early spring, try to be sure the winds will be in your favor even in late autumn, when prevailing winds normally begin reversing direction to blow from the northwest.

A Final Word of Caution: Your Safety

Cannabis growing has become a large and very much thug-run business in the past few decades. No grower of any size crop welcomes strangers stumbling onto his plants,

but there are large illegal operations, some of which have been growing perhaps hundreds of pounds of commercial bud for many years, that regard trespassers as outright threats to their profits. There is no "wild" cannabis in most of the United States, and any plants you might encounter off the beaten track are being tended by someone— someone who might be close by and armed, or who might have strung plants and their perimeters with booby traps. If you do happen upon someone else's crop—I've done it while scouting for new places to grow my own—the best strategy, ethically and prudently, is to immediately leave the area. And as you leave, keep an eye out for fishhooks strung every foot or so on long lengths of fishing line that has been hung—often at face level—from branches and shrubs. Be alert for the dreaded punji board of 2x6 planks hammered full of long nails. Move slowly, always looking in all directions before taking a step for triplines strung at any level, sticks and branches whose orientation seems out of place against their surroundings, and any piece of wood that has been whittled. As exactly as you can, take the same route back out that brought you to find the plants; if that isn't possible, then absolutely avoid any established trails that might be strung with booby traps that the people who set them know to avoid. So long as marijuana is stricken with an illegal status in any state, and so long as that status keeps the black-market cost at more than $1,000 per pound, large pot crops are sure to be fiercely protected from thieves. My point isn't to scare you, just to prompt you to ask yourself how many thousands of dollars that any crop you find accidentally might be worth, and then estimate how many outlaw growers would go to dangerous lengths to protect their profit. To prove that point dramatically, a man named Stanley Wallace was only recently shot and killed while allegedly stealing marijuana from a legal, fenced-in private garden planted with medicinal pot in California's central Fresno County.

CHAPTER 6

Watering and Pruning

Step Six: Creating a healthy crop of marijuana involves more than just getting your plants in the dirt. Now is the time to vigilantly provide enough water for your crop while keeping the plants fit and trim through judicious pruning.

Focus Points:
- Watering Your Crop
- Pruning Leaves
- Dangers of Overpruning

It's no small feat to successfully coax your marijuana plants to life and then give them a permanent home. Now that you're officially farming your own crop, you want to make sure all that hard work doesn't go to waste by losing your plants before they reach maturity. Again, this is ultimately a "back to basics" issue. Faithful watering and judicious pruning are the two keys to ensure a thriving crop of harvestable marijuana plants.

Watering Your Crop

There is a fairly widespread belief that because cannabis grows in Mexico—and Mexico, according to all the cowboy movies, is desert—the plants can live with little water. The truth is that marijuana plants like water as much as the next species, and growers should anticipate that as plants grow in height and produce more foliage, they will need progressively more water to maintain good health. By the time your plants are 3 feet tall or higher, they will need about 1 gallon of water per plant per day.

This is where good planning and site selection pay off. Unless you've had the good fortune to plant on a streambank or some other location where the water table is near

Note the stub of the shade leaf that spawned the lush, full branches sprouting from the apex of leaf stem and plant stalk.

Despite its apparent good health and strength, this still-unbranched cannabis plant is too small to be pruned yet.

enough to the surface for plants to draw their own water, they are likely to need daily watering during the hottest and driest days of summer—July and August in most of North America.

Pruning Leaves

One of the perks of growing your own pot is that you can enjoy some of the benefits even before plants have begun to show their gender. Some pot farmers subscribe to a hands-off philosophy, refusing to trim plants and just letting nature take its course. My experience has led me to a few different conclusions that cause me to believe that controlled pruning is critical to achieving maximum health, growth, and THC content.

"Pruning" is the basic process in which a plant cultivator cuts off dead (or even still live) pieces of a plant. The idea is that by taking away a minimal amount of material, the grower is actually helping ensure the survival of the overall plant.

Pruning away pale, yellowing, or brown-tipped leaves cleanly with scissors or a sharp knife is something like excising dying tissue from human wounds. Yellowed, dead

The large shade (or "sun") leaves that feed the branches that grow from their stem joints can be removed—judiciously—to both accelerate plant growth, and to encourage production of insect-repellant THC.

With a healthy branch sprouting from its apex, this shade leaf can be removed.

leaves are a fact of life as lower branches are shaded out by increasing foliage density above. As long as dying leaves are attached to the parent plant, they drain some of its resources. Affected leaves detach at their stems' bases and fall off eventually, but a clean snip of the stem on a leaf that shows signs of dying is less taxing to the parent plant than supporting a slowly dying leaf for weeks on end. More resources are channeled into new growth, resulting in larger, healthier plants at maturity.

Pruning also enhances growth by promoting the formation of new branches. When a seedling reaches its tough, energetic stage, when it has at least eight pairs of lobed leaves, you should begin to see green hairlike growths sprouting from the bases of leaf stems where they meet the main stalk. At this point the plant should be sprouting a pair of new leaves from its top every day, some of which may be as large as a man's hand, and each uppermost leaf will sprout a pair of these fledgling branches. More branches mean

As branches grow longer, innermost leaves will be shaded, will turn yellow and fall off, and should be removed to help direct a plant's resources to where they're needed most.

This well-pruned prebudding adult shows how leaving just the topmost tiers of shade leaves is sufficient to power large plants, while having pruned those before them causes a plant to become bushy and full.

more buds, and as soon as the pair of young branches begin to sprout their own leaves from either side, I remove the large five- or seven-lobed "shade" leaf that spawned them.

Left to themselves, the shade leaves will turn yellow and fall off anyway when the branches from their bases begin sprouting their own leaves; by pruning the shade leaves early, I keep plants struggling enough to maximize growth during a short growing season, but not so much that their resources are taxed. Like a human bodybuilder, the goal is to grow healthy, strong tissue through stress, while feeding a subject the nutrients needed to make the entire stronger and tougher. I take only the largest leaves—at least 4 inches long, discounting stem—and only those with healthy branches already started from their bases. This opens the smaller leaves below those large leaves to more sunlight, while also forcing them to grow and make up for the chlorophyll production lost by removal of the shade leaves.

Another method of spurring branch growth is to remove the top and the ends of branches. In most instances "topping" plants and branch tips does promote the growth of branches, but it also retards further length until the nipped end heals and sprouts a fork of two new end branches. Proponents of this practice argue that topping makes a plant thicker and bushier, with more leaves. My feeling is that the retardation of length growth isn't offset by the increase in new branch growth, nor does topping result in markedly more leaf growth.

Dangers of Overpruning

Overpruning is a very common mistake, and an understandable one; once your very own pot leaves have achieved a THC level sufficient to make an average smoker slack-jaw stoned, then it's pretty tempting to enjoy it more frequently than you might the pot that came from a purchased bag. That's great, and it's fun to share the fruits of your labors with friends, but always bear in mind that the best is yet to come, when the females give you big, fat, sticky buds that get the job done within three tokes. It pays—literally—to do nothing that might hinder a plant's summer growing stage, which could also take away from its later fruiting stage.

Following the directions already given about pruning leaves will help you to avoid overpruning, but here are a few rules of thumb: Never take a leaf that doesn't have branches sprouting from its basal stem; never take all of the leaves from any stalk or branch; never tear leaf stems free, but always cut them with a sharp knife or scissors; always water a plant immediately after you've pruned it—preferably with plant food—to lessen the shock and to spur new growth.

This chain-link enclosure protects the plant inside from herbivores that might eat it, and the chain-link can be used to help spread branches to achieve maximum growth.

You will probably prune a lot of leaves from your plants through the summer months, and I regret to admit that they will probably not be worth smoking until your plants are three months old. It will probably take that long for plants to achieve their peak insect-repelling THC levels, a cycle that roughly and not coincidently corresponds to the life cycles of leaf-eating insects. If a plant has been carefully pruned and mildly tormented, its leaves will have acquired sufficient THC to make them definitely worth smoking by mid-July. It doesn't hurt to test-smoke a few leaves prior to that, just to see if you've gotten lucky, but in most cases you'll end up throwing away pruned leaves for about the first three months because they simply won't get you high. Discard these impotent leaves, preferably in a fire, because one thing worse than getting busted for possession of marijuana is getting busted for possessing lousy marijuana.

Placing pruned leaves in a sealed ziplock bag overnight before drying causes them to manufacture sugars that make the cannabis sweeter-tasting and gentler to smoke.

Despite its good looks, this leaf has little THC content; that will increase as the plant is continually pruned.

It's enough to make a dedicated toker cry, but I've seen large, mature pot plants that had grown to adulthood without proper tending, and whose THC levels were so low that even the buds weren't worth smoking. Over the years, I've developed a theory that judicious pruning can actually increase the tetrahydrocannabinol (THC) levels produced by a growing plant.

It appears that THC, like the oils in catnip that make cats go euphoric, is in fact an insect repellant. Only a few insects will eat marijuana in its branching stage, and then usually only lightly (the exception being slugs) because the bugs literally appear to be stoned. Strategic trimming, just enough to keep a plant struggling slightly, can inhance its production of natural insect repellant to pretty impressive levels.

Visual indicators of leaves that need pruning include brown tips, yellowing, half-devoured lobes, and any sign of withering. Also remove any leaves with branches starting from their bases, taking the topmost leaves first to drive smaller leaves below to grow faster.

CHAPTER 7

Hazards to Your Plants

Step Seven: As with every other living object on the planet, marijuana plants are susceptible to unique hazards and illnesses. No matter how much TLC you lavish on your crop, you are eventually going to encounter some type of threat or problem to your plants. This chapter is designed to give you an idea of the problems you might face as either an indoor or outdoor grower, and to offer some hints on how to overcome the most common obstacles.

Focus Points:
- Indoor and Outdoor Health: Common Symptoms of Illness
- Outdoor Dangers: Common Pests and Problems
- Indoor Hazards: Grow-Room Pests

Indoor and Outdoor Health: Common Symptoms of Illness

Before a leafing marijuana plant dies, it will usually give plenty of notice that it's ailing with a range of visible symptoms. In many cases a specific ailment can be identified, and efficiently treated, by knowing which symptoms match up to the most common ailments.

Problem: Larger, mature leaves are turning yellowish, but smaller still-growing leaves are green.

Answer: Nitrogen deficiency; add nitrate of soda or any good commercial bag fertilizer. An effective home remedy is use nitrogen urea (pee), in the unscientific solution of one bladderfull per gallon of water.

Problem: Mature leaves become yellowish in small-veined areas.

Answer: Magnesium deficiency; this is most simply addressed by using a good commercial fertilizer, or replanting in a bed of topsoil or thoroughly composted manure.

Problem: Mature leaves turn yellow, with edges mottled with dark gray spots.

Answer: Potassium deficiency; add muriate of potash, or a mix of one-half cup of wood ashes in a gallon of unchlorinated water.

Problem: Weak support structure; stems and branches that crack, split, and break apart easily at the crotches.

Answer: Boron deficiency; add any commercial plant food containing boron.

Problem: Small wrinkled leaves that fail to fully unfurl, with yellowed veins.

Answer: Zinc deficiency; add plant food with zinc.

Problem: Young leaves grow stunted and deformed, often turning yellow and falling off.

Answer: Molybdenum deficiency; add a good plant food containing molybdenum.

Problem: *Leaves begin turning yellow at their outer ends, with tips dying and becoming curled and brown.*

Answer: *Too much water; this problem is seldom seen with plants growing on open ground, but can occur with potted plants, especially young ones.*

Outdoor Dangers: Common Pests and Problems

Attrition rates for fledgling plants are often terrible for outdoor growers—more than 50 percent in some cases—and whether most plants live or die is a daily challenge until they're at least two months old and a foot high or more. Even then there may be dangers from slugs, whose very passage across foliage leaves it dead and fouled with mucus, or even deer, elk, and moose that can (and do) wipe out more than a dozen large plants in a single night. And then of course there are people; reapers who will make off with

Overwatering is a problem that exists mostly in indoor grow rooms; symptoms include a yellowing, then dying of leaf tips.

all the plants that they can carry, regardless of their stage of growth, and sharp-eyed drug cops who live to be on the evening news next to a pile of burning marijuana plants (not a bad place to stand, actually). Outdoor growers contend with a number of natural threats to their crops, but most threats can be dealt with effectively. Following are some of the more common pests a grower can expect to encounter.

Grasshoppers and leafhoppers are among the few leaf-eating insects that seem able to subsist on hemp foliage. Beginning at the edges, both of these insects eat away narrow strips of leaf until sometimes there's nothing left except the heaviest veins. In fact, though, these bugs don't usually eat much, and it's almost worth it to see the little critters so stoned that sometimes you can pluck them from a leaf. If either should become a problem, I lightly spray a perimeter of permethrin-based insect repellant onto the ground around the plant out to a radius of 6 feet. This synthetic pyrethrin—a product of the daisy family—is relatively safe to humans, and is the active ingredient in pet flea sprays, but kills insects and arachnids on contact. I don't recommend using it on any part of the plant, but a perimeter of permethrin on the ground is sufficient to discourage most plant-eaters (even mammals) for a period of at least three days. Permethrin has no lasting effects on a plant or to the environment.

Slugs can be a serious threat to marijuana plants, especially during wet, warm summer nights when they emerge from beneath damp, rotting logs and stumps to find food.

Left unchecked, just a half dozen of these lowly foragers can climb the stalk of a 3-foot plant, consume a surprising amount of leaf material, and inflict real injury to the plant. For a reason I don't know, the slime trail a slug leaves across marijuana leaves is sufficient to kill those leaves by itself. Worse, slugs seem drawn to tender branch ends, which their browsing kills. And since branch ends are where most growth occurs—including buds—it becomes imperative to stop invading slugs before they kill entire plants.

Once again, a skirt of permethrin sprayed onto the ground around plants is an effective wall against slugs, which react immediately and violently when they touch it. If possible, visit your plants after dark, when slugs are most active, and use a dim flashlight or headlamp to pluck any that you find from plants using your fingers. You might drop the repulsive creatures into a jar for relocation to a less objectionable location, but I generally pull them from a plant and fling them into the woods. The

Garden slugs can be a serious hazard; they are voracious eaters of marijuana, and their slime trails kill all that they touch.

airborne relocation does no harm to the slug, but I know it won't be back tonight, while a shield of permethrin ensures that it won't return after that.

Deer usually leave marijuana plants alone, but like squirrels that regularly nibble hallucinogenic mushrooms, there are a few cervid stoners that enjoy being high, and these individuals may strip an entire plant. Lacking upper incisors, deer (cattle too) with a taste for pot take branches between their lower incisors and hard upper palate and pull backward, stripping off all the foliage from that branch. Left unchecked, a single deer can completely defoliate two or more 4-foot plants in a single night.

Some large-scale growers for whom healthy plants mean income claim that the very best repellant for deer in the dope field is deer blood—and as a bonus you get to eat the deer that was made an example of. Less violent repellants can be as simple as depositing your own urine onto trees and shrubs to demonstrate that you are the dominant predator (vegans aside, all animals regard humans as meat-eaters). This is my preferred animal-repellant method. Should deer become too numerous and too pushy, urine scents sold in hunting supply stores and marketed for hunting work well if used judiciously; white-tailed deer will avoid the scent of a dominant moose or a sow bear, as will most animals.

Other animals, from mice and chipmunks to some birds, eat marijuana shoots and tender young plants before their stalks become woody and their THC content gets too high. Smaller animals also respect human scent-posts of urine, but the best method for

Mottled yellow-brown spots on this cannabis leaf were made by feeding spider mites.

frightening off the little guys is the scent of a predator built by nature to hunt them, like fox or coyote scent, which is sold online at www.buckstopscents.com and other manufacturer Web sites.

Spider mites and **other parasitic bugs** that feed and reside on growing marijuana plants are seldom a problem when growing outdoors. Should mites or aphids invade your plants, it goes without saying that conventional spray-on insecticides are not a viable option for foliage that will find its way into a human body. Closet growers have had good luck spraying leaves and branches of infested plants with a solution of fresh garlic and water steeped to make a tea that does no harm to plants but is apparently repugnant to most parasites.

Gypsy moth caterpillars, known colloquially as **"armyworms,"** are common across America, and their large webbed habitats in tree crotches are a common summer sight, especially in cherry and other fruit trees, and particularly when populations are at their cyclical high. The caterpillars, which have almost no natural enemies because they just

This is awful; dead spider mite carcasses deeply entrenched inside a bud can render it foul-tasting and unsmokable.

Spider mites are the worst predator of cannabis plants, but they are rarely seen on plants growing outdoors.

taste bad, may become voracious during these peaks, because they have literally eaten themselves into mass starvation.

Population "seasons" that wax and wane like this are found throughout nature, and when starving overpopulated caterpillars are driven to feed and propagate under conditions that are simply inadequate to support their numbers, plants and trees that are not normally food will be razed as well. Again, a perimeter of permethrin sprayed onto the ground for a distance of about 6 feet all around is an effective deterrent, but it might need to be reapplied every two or three days and soon after every rain. By experimenting, I've also had good results from surrounding plants with a thin layer of fresh cow manure; for whatever reason, armyworms seem unwilling to crawl across fresh poop. Worms that do make it onto your plants are most effectively dealt with by plucking them off by hand the way farmers of old did before insecticides and crushing them underfoot—that practice might not set well with some folks, but what are you going to do, relocate the caterpillars?

Black widow spiders seem to have an unusual affinity for pot plants. I can't say why, but I can relate several midsummer experiences when I've found an elegant female black widow perched on a web she'd anchored to the branches of a large marijuana plant. I leave them alone until harvesttime, but I advise plucking a widow-inhabited plant with caution, especially when a protective mother is guarding a roundish egg casing suspended in her web.

Indoor Hazards: Grow-Room Pests

Probably the worst pest of closet-grown plants is the red spider mite, a tiny scarlet arachnid. These parasites can do great damage to your plants by feeding on their fluids and then wrapping leaves into tunnel-like breeding chambers where new mites hatch by the tens of thousands. Unchecked, the minute marauders can kill an entire grow room of the largest plants.

Yet, a potentially serious invasion of spider mites cannot be resolved with off-the-shelf pesticides that are poisonous to every living thing. Growers have had good luck with spraying mites with a mix of 20:1 tap water and dishwashing liquid. I've also had good results from a mist of strong garlic tea sprayed directly onto the bugs. Neither of these treatments does any harm to the plants, and neither are especially toxic, but I think it's a good idea to mist plants daily with plain water for about a week after mites have been eradicated to wash them clean again.

PART THREE

Completing the Growing Process—

DETERMINE GENDER, CLONE YOUR PLANTS, AND HARVEST YOUR CROP

CHAPTER 8

Determining Gender and Tailoring Bud Growth

Step Eight: **Before you can enjoy the fruits of your labor, you need to know what to expect from what you've got. This chapter is designed to help you cultivate the most potent crop possible by first allowing you to accurately identify what types of plants you have and where you need to stimulate further growth.**

Focus Points:
- **Sexing Your Plant**
- **Seeds or No Seeds?**
- **Buds and Gender: Identifying the Best Product**
- **Accelerating Female Bud Growth**
- **Nurturing Buds in General**

Up to this point, your growing project has been solely focused on fulfilling practical necessities that will ensure the survival of your plants. Using patience, skill, and a little bit of luck, you should have spent the last six to eight weeks watching tiny seeds grow from fragile-looking seedlings into leafy thriving marijuana plants. Now that your crop is thriving, it's time to turn your attention to the future. Maintaining your garden, deciding when to harvest, and even planning for next year's crop are all issues that are directly affected by each individual plant's gender.

As your plant matures (and you get one step closer to that first satisfying puff on the most delicious, home-grown, and pampered pot you've ever smoked) you will start to notice changes in foliage production and developing appendages. Small growths will appear at the juncture where leaf stems connect to plant stalks. Certain plants will grow taller and thinner while others will remain short but bushy. These changes are a direct result of the plants reaching a new level of growth in which they are sexually mature.

Still immature, this top bud, or spike, is unmistakable.

Once plants begin to show signs of their gender, you can better identify which plants will be more potent and which plants you wish to reproduce to keep you smoking throughout the year.

Sexing Your Plant

Like most plants, cannabis is photosensitive, growing in different ways in response to lengthening, then shortening summer days. When changing seasons cause daylight hours to drop below eighteen hours, marijuana plants are triggered to enter their "flowering" (also known as "fruiting") phase. Male plants react first and fastest, producing "false" buds with tiny green-white egg-shaped flowers that visibly emit a cloud of pollen when shaken.

The top bud of a preflowering male can be a sweet and potent smoke.

Females trail males by about two weeks, finally showing their gender by developing a growth at the ends of the top and each branch that resembles a tiny whitish-haired cactus. In another month those infant buds will have taken on considerable mass, their outsides will be sticky with resin, and they will give off strong odors that may range (presuming your seeds were culled from "commercial" pot) from very skunklike to a sweet, even pleasant bruised-fruit odor.

Before waning daylight forces cannabis plants to openly reveal their gender, a good rule of thumb is to anticipate that your tallest plants are likely to be males. Beginning pot farmers usually find that revelation to be depressing, but male plants have evolved to grow faster and taller and to mature before females. By towering over females, male flowers can drop pollen down onto budding females, and the tiny granules will travel farther on a breeze.

Males also die more quickly, sometimes before the first frost, and until they do, the flowers they produce can be snipped off, dried, and smoked (or eaten) to produce a high that is nearly as good as the one gotten from smoking bud (for more information on harvesting and preparing marijuana, see **Chapters Eleven** and **Twelve**). A male's flowering stage can be prolonged by trimming several inches from the tops and ends of branches, leaving some flower-bearing stalks below to regrow into more "male buds" that can be harvested and smoked.

Seeds or No Seeds?

As the existence of genders implies, marijuana plants in the wild reproduce when male pollen fertilizes female flowers and the next generation of seeds are produced. As a grower you have to decide if you want to allow some of your plants to develop seeds or if you want to keep your crop unfertilized so that your plants remain unaffected by the chemical changes caused by reproduction.

Seeds can be a tricky issue for home growers. It's a definite bonus to have your own stash of seeds for planting next year's crop, but reproducing can have adverse effects on several characteristics of the female plant.

As soon as a female plant is fertilized, the production of resin (which contains significant concentrations of THC compound) begins to slow down as the plant concentrates on producing seeds. In contrast, the "bud" of an unfertilized female flower is the most

The small green nodules on this male bud are unopened flowers.

Male cannabis plants typically grow faster and taller and flower earlier than females.

potent part of any marijuana plant. Even more important, a female plant can stay in the "flowering" stage for six to ten weeks as long as no fertilization takes place. This unfertilized state results in the growth of numerous buds all over a healthy female plant.

Many urban legends surround the topic of seedless "ganja." Seedless buds are easier to deal with because there's no need to painstakingly remove foul-tasting seeds that might be inadvertently rolled into a joint or stuffed into a bowl. Pot growers who

Pot smokers are primarily interested in the buds produced by female plants, because buds can contain several times the concentration of tetrahydrocannabinol (THC) found in leaves. That does not, however, mean that only female buds can get you high. As explained earlier, by judiciously pruning your plants during the summer to simulate assault by leaf-eating insects, you can induce an overall increase in the level of insect-repelling THC it generates throughout the summer leaf-growing period and into the autumn budding stage. THC levels rise slowly at first, so try not to be disappointed when your first cuttings have the potency of grass clippings. Pruned leaves should become potent enough to smoke by July (assuming a March sprouting), inducing a slack-jawed type of body buzz after a half dozen or more hits. Many people prefer to dry leaves and then powder them in a coffee grinder to make a "pot flour" that can be blended fifty-fifty with white flour to make cookies, cakes, brownies, even pancakes and waffles (recipes are given at the end of this book).

A male *indica* plant in full flower.

The shorter male on the left has flowered, and now its leaves have turned purple prior to turning yellow and dying; contrast this with the green budding females around it.

bootleg their crops like seeds because they add weight. After that, as the weed makes its way through the marketing process, the value-subtracted effect of seeds on profit is passed on until only the terminal buyer, the user, pays for pot seeds he can't smoke.

If you prefer the convenience of ganja—no seeds, just peel a bud from its stem and stuff it into a paper or a bowl—then you'll want to uproot male plants as soon as they begin to grow flower buds at the tops and at the ends of their branches. Ideally, this will be done before the first pollen-bearing flowers appear.

Males are always the first to reveal their gender, beginning with tiny flower buds at the ends of their branches and tops that might be mistaken for the female buds that are the real prime smoke in terms of potency, fragrance, and taste. It takes a trained eye to confidently rip out large, healthy male plants at the first sign of a bud; no horror could be greater than to kill a 4-foot female that would potentially produce 2 ounces of lovely

buds. And because male plants begin emitting pollen granules as soon as they bud, even before they actually flower, the most earnest attempt at producing pure, seedless buds ends up with a few seeds.

Fortunately for this book, there are seeds in most "street" marijuana, because to prove a point, every plant shown on

The top bud of a female plant in September

these pages was sprouted from seeds culled from a half ounce of pot I bought from a local seller. There are nine females out of eighteen adults in this crop, which is below the 70 percent male average. Like most personal-use growers, I let the males pollinate the buds, and when this harvest comes in there will be more seeds than I'll want to plant.

Buds and Gender: Identifying the Best Product

As mentioned earlier, the bud of a marijuana plant is the prized appendage that appears after a plant enters the flowering stage of its life cycle (see "Marijuana Life Cycle" at the beginning of this book). The leaves of the marijuana plant contain THC, but the buds of both male and female plants are the most potent product by far. So as an individual grower, it's important to focus a significant amount of attention on the buds of your crop.

Budding, in general, is an exciting time, because it is the stage of growth that says you've succeeded at producing a viable commodity. It's a pioneer kind of emotion, with a feeling of satisfaction that has always gone hand in hand with knowing a person can fend for himself or herself.

Male Buds

As a personal-use grower, you'll probably want to harvest the seeds for next year's crop along with the bud you smoke. For that reason—and because you don't have to buy them by weight at premium prices in a bag of what should contain only smokable bud—you'll want your males to pollinate females and produce viable seeds.

If your seeds—like those that grew the crop illustrated here—were culled from a bag of street-purchased marijuana, be prepared to see widely varying growth forms. While there are bona fide connoisseurs who grow highly specialized selectively bred plants with THC levels higher than anything ever

A flowered male in a drying shed.

Students of survival may also recognize that during a global disaster marijuana will almost certainly become a form of currency in the barter economy that follows just a few days after loss of services and utilities. Sadly, and ironically, marijuana could become a welcome drug for pain management, dementia, and other trauma that follow the aftermath of disaster. Were I to survive a terrible disaster like the Haitian earthquake, and even if I were completely unharmed, I'd want an adequate supply of good dope just to take the edge off a shockingly terrible reality.

grown by nature, those champagne marijuanas are not what you can expect to buy from local dealers. Fortunately, male flowers and female buds are recognizably similar in every species, even after extensive hybridization, and once the plants make manifest their genders with true buds and flowers, it's easy to distinguish between them.

Despite a widely believed myth that male plants lack the THC levels to be smoke-worthy, many a toker has been stoned to happiness by midsummer leaves snipped from typically vigorous males that have been manicured just enough to pique THC (insect repellant) production. Even more potent are the male "buds," which are in fact buds only in the sense that they sprout short branches of tiny roundish pollen-laden flowers.

Female Buds

Females show their sex one to two weeks after males; this is nature's way of ensuring that males will be in full flower and generating maximum pollen when their own

Preflower male buds.

sticky buds emerge to trap wind-carried granules that will pollinate them and produce fertile seeds. "Budlings" reveal themselves as round, whitish, hairy growths at the tip of each branch and top. As top buds grow longer, less robust buds begin to sprout below from leaf intersections. Kept healthy, well-watered, and left to fully mature, the smaller buds can achieve lengths of more than 2 inches, turning branches, and especially tops, into a continuous, solid covering of smaller buds along a main stalk, terminating into a longer, spiky bud at their tips. Trimmed of larger leaves, these beautiful long bud colonies have been sold as Thai Stick, but unlike the real thing they are not usually treated with tincture of opium (smoking authentic Thai Stick requires a place to lie down for a while, as I recall).

Accelerating Female Bud Growth

When female cannabis plants begin to fruit, you'll see little hairy buds emerging from each intersection of leaf and branch, branch and stem. Under the best conditions, "budlets" sprouting along the length of a branch or stem will grow longer and fatter until its entire length is covered in masses of bud, terminating in a usually impressive spike of top bud.

In addition, when your female cannabis plants begin to bud, you'll note color changes in their leaves. Many will turn yellow, die, and fall off. Some will turn purple, even red, as days get shorter and nights turn colder (if you're an outdoor grower). Take the yellow leaves, and any leaves that are turning yellow, to make the plant focus more energies on growing its buds. Don't discard yellowed or browned leaves, though. They'll come in handy for recipes later, and if you should run out of bud, properly cured leaves can be smoked to stave off cravings for THC.

Short growing seasons, like necessity itself, can be the proverbial mother of invention. One year when I enjoyed an especially good crop, with twenty-two budding females of a dozen strains, each of which produced between ½ ounce and 3 ounces of bud in a variety of flavors, I experimented with pruning buds to accelerate growth. It began when the top bud-spikes on some of the larger (5-foot or taller) plants began to show prominently as changing autumn leaves first contrasted against the plants' bright green, then fell to earth, leaving them exposed against a landscape of browning vegetation.

Although male buds are sometimes mistaken for females at the start of the autumn flowering season, there is no mistaking the hairy star of beginning bud.

Fearing that some grouse or rabbit hunter might stumble onto the site and recognize the very prominent spikes, I sliced each top bud from its stalk with my knife and took them all home to be dried and smoked. I figured that even if some opportunistic reaper did steal my crop, I had at least saved several ounces of the best and biggest buds.

As the topped female plants continued to flower, the lower, smaller buds seemed to be spurred to grow at an accelerated rate, as though trying to compensate for the loss of their bud spikes. With some trepidation, I took the tips from some of the branch buds, and the buds below them also grew faster. Now the practice of trimming bud spikes and branch ends to make those below them grow bigger and faster (and maybe even more potent) is a part of my preharvest routine.

Nurturing Buds in General

As mentioned previously, plants your pot garden produces with seeds culled from a bag of street marijuana may vary noticeably because the plants they came from were of different species and strains. I actually kind of like this grab bag of mixed genes, because you never know when you're planting just what will come up—as I stated at the beginning of this book, personal-use growing should be fun. The seeds you plant may produce many different types of buds, like white-haired Super Skunk, the bluish "pine tree" growth of Aussie Blue, leafy green Easy Rider, or the superdense, all-bud Light of Jah, to name just a few of the strains you're likely to produce growing seeds culled from a single ounce of commercial pot.

Within these there are even more variations of taste and odor. I love the fragrance of growing marijuana buds, from the startlingly musky aroma of the skunkiest *sativa* to the almost appetite-inducing smell of "bubblegum" buds, some of which really do smell like Bazooka bubblegum. One trait that all of them share at maturity is an ability to get you stoned with just a few tokes. Fragrance probably has little to do with potency—unless you believe that you can smell THC—but I like to separate one or two especially fragrant plants from the rest for special occasions. During the October–November harvesttime I feel kind of like a kid at Christmas, sniffing among the different plants to decide which one I want to smoke first. It's a great feeling that I recommend for every marijuana grower.

Budding plants need less of the nitrogen that is so necessary to summer leaf and branch growth. Phosphorous is the nutrient most needed to make

Just starting to bud, this female top will become a long, thick spike of buds in about a month.

buds be all they can be, and expert growers generally concur that a plant-food mix of 10 percent nitrogen, 30 percent phosphorous, and 10 percent potassium is the best mix for maximum bud growth. This formula is abbreviated, and known by gardening store employees, as NPK 10–30–10. In recent years phosphorous has been all but banned in detergents and soaps, but in times past—like 1967, when laundry soaps contained 9.4 percent phosphorous—a tablespoonful of Tide in a gallon of water was a great home-brewed solution to maximizing bud growth. There is also a useful percentage of phosphorous in the ashes of most woods, and ash, mixed well at a half-cup to a gallon of water, can also help to grow bigger buds.

The thousands of pounds of smuggled pot seized by authorities represents a small percentage of the amount actually smuggled across American borders from both Canada and Mexico, and that is pertinent because very large crops cannot receive the individual attention of personal-use plots. Dried brown buds repackaged from vacuum-sealed 1-pound bags look pretty much the same, but it's probable that the ounce you purchased contains buds from a dozen different plants, and perhaps as many strains. For-profit farmers don't care if the buds they dry and package are from *sativas*, *indicas*, or the latest Amsterdam hybrid, because they know that all mature buds will get a smoker high.

CHAPTER 9

Cloning

Step Nine: **Although not a necessary step in growing marijuana, cloning is an incredibly useful skill for any horticulturalist. Once mastered, cloning will allow you to increase your yield without having to compromise potency or risk reproductive issues.**

Focus Points:
- **The Cloning Concept**
- **Methods**
- **Transplanting Clones**
- **How to Clone Like a Pro**

Lets face it, at this point you know which plants in your garden are male and female. You know which are sickly and which have thrived. You may have even sampled a few buds from your garden as you've gone along and recognized a superior buzz from a more mundane producer. Chances are at this point there is at least one "favorite" plant you just wish would grow infinitely in your backyard (who said pot growing had to be egalitarian?).

Cloning in a grow room under controlled conditions is usually more successful than cloning outdoors, as these young clones show

Through there are no guarantees when growing marijuana, there is a tried-and-true method for reproducing your most successful plants without having to go through the process of fertilization and seed reproduction. "Cloning" is a simple method that allows you to grow any plant by taking a clipping from a mature plant and basically allowing it to grow into its own. As you continue to perfect your gardening technique, cloning is a skill that will come up often and serve you infinitely well over the course of your growing career.

The Cloning Concept

Probably everyone with a grandma or aunt has seen cloning performed when one of them snipped a shoot from someone's potted plant and dropped the cut end into a water glass half filled with water. Both were then left sitting on a windowsill until the submerged, cut end sprouted new roots and could be transplanted into soil. Grandma made it look effortless.

The advantage of cloning for those who have the knack for it is that it theoretically permits a grower to expand his crop geometrically—especially in places with long growing seasons—because lower branches that often die from being shaded can be sliced off and nurtured into becoming a whole new plant. Being taken from plants that are already three months into the growing season, clones that take another month to grow roots cannot be expected to achieve maximum growth. But each female can grow a 10-inch, half-ounce, all-bud top, even if the plant itself is only a foot tall. If you have ten plants, and can clone just four lower branches from each plant, you've probably at least doubled your bud harvest.

The downside is that in most cases with most growers, most clones die before they grow roots and become new plants. I've tried using rooting compounds, not using them, different soil combinations, etcetera. My personal success rate with clones runs about 7 percent, so if I start twenty clones, it's with the expectation that only one or two will survive, and if I'm lucky one of those will be female.

Methods

For the clone masters, the procedure consists of cutting the last 10 inches from the end of a lower branch, leaving at least one pair of leaves from which to sprout a pair of new branches. Cutting clones from the parent plant requires a very sharp knife and a steeply angled cut diagonally across the stem to expose the broadest area possible to the growing medium and maximize the potential for root growth from the slice area. Remove all developed leaves from the clone's stalk to enable it to focus its entire energy on growing new roots, but take care not to harm the delicate and critical top.

A good rooting compound isn't absolutely necessary, but it definitely increases your chances of growing successful clones.

The experts simply dip the wetted sliced end into rooting compound powder—available at most garden supply centers—and shove the cut stem down into saturated potting soil, where it takes root. Most of my own clones die before taking root with this method, and those that take root take so long to do it that the growing season is nearly over by the time they start to grow.

My best luck at cloning has come from following Grandma's example with cuttings half immersed in water treated with plant food. Except that where she used a water tumbler, I prefer to use a plastic 16-ounce soda bottle; the container is rugged and cheap, and the bottle's narrow neck helps to keep clones standing upright while also inhibiting the evaporation of water from inside the bottle. Agitate the submerged stems every few days to dislodge algae, and change the water if algae becomes prevalent. Again, remove all leaves from the stalk, but be careful to not harm its top. Subdued sunlight is best for clones until they noticeably begin to grow new leaves from their tops, which will also usually coincide with the development of a healthy root ball that is ready to transplant.

Transplanting Clones

Clones that have rooted in soils can be transplanted using the same procedure for transplanting seedlings that was described earlier (see **Chapter Two** and **Chapter Five** for more information). Transplanting water-rooted clones means transporting the containers that hold them, water and all, to the transplant site. This can be a giant inconvenience if you have lots of clones and the transplant location is far away, but it's imperative that the clones' delicate new roots are not exposed to air, which could kill them.

First, ready a site with a hole about 1 foot wide by 1 foot deep to receive the clone, but fill in the hole around the plant with a blend of potting soil and excavated dirt. Press soil around the plant downward with firm but not hard pressure to help secure its root system. Finally, water soil around the plant base thoroughly with at least a half gallon of water treated with plant food. Having been hardened adults when they were taken from their parent plant, clones are very tough once they take root; barring natural disasters or foul play, a clone transplanted in July will begin to flower in late August or September.

A word of caution: Don't be surprised if the sex of a clone is different than the sex of the plant it was cut from.

How to Clone Like a Pro

The following cloning instructions were provided by a cloning pro who prefers to be identified by the pseudonym Hick. Based on his results, and the results of other growers who've used the advice given below, following these instructions will result in healthy clones that develop roots quickly and hit the ground running after transplanting.

(A)   Supplies—"KISS" (Keep It Simple, Stupid). I don't use a lot of extras or specialties. Equal parts vermiculite/perlite/quality potting soil, I prefer Black Gold, but everyone has a preference. I advise NOT to use anything with added/time release fertilizers. Any quality rooting hormone, I happen to be using Green Light, but Rootone, Olivias, or another brand should work as well. I use 8-ounce plastic cups with eight to ten drainage holes in their bottoms. A new, sterilized razor knife. Sharp scissors for various trimming operations.

(B)   Medium preparation—I put the pots or cups to set in a pan of pH-adjusted water. Letting them absorb from the bottom up ensures full, equal saturation. Vermiculite and peat tend to float and allow water to run straight through without good saturation when the medium is this light, so watering potted clones from the top is not recommended.

(C)   Donor mothers should be prepped a few hours prior to pruning with a soaking watering of Age Old Bloom 5–10–5. High Phosphate promotes rooting, as well as flowering. I believe the donor's health is possibly the single most important factor in growing successful clones.

(D)   Take likely clone candidates from branches that are midway up the donor plant; I like to start with shoots at least 4 inches long.

(E)   Cut stem cleanly at 45 degrees with a sharp knife—not scissors.

(F) Trim lower leaves from clone cutting; the nubs where leaves have been taken provide growth spots for roots to start, so scraping or scarification of the stem is not needed.

(H) Hydrate cuttings in a weak kelp solution to relax them prior to planting; I like to let them soak for fifteen to thirty minutes.

(I) A final cut is made at a 45-degree angle while the stem is submerged; cutting the stem underwater helps to prevent an air bubble from forming over and blocking nutrients from entering the stem's arteries.

(J) Rooting hormone—make sure the cut is well coated. I remove excess by tapping the cutting briskly with a flick of the finger.

(K) Cups filled with potting soil and vermiculite/perlite, presaturated and ready, with finger-size holes pressed into holes large enough to accommodate the cutting without scraping off the rooting hormone.

(L) Planting—holes should be large enough that the stem slips easily in without scraping off the rooting hormone.

(M) Planted—press the medium firmly around the stem; contact with the stem is vital for rooting.

(N) Final step—I use Plexiglas on top of the Tupperware container as a humidity dome. Remove it twice a day, for an hour or so, every day extending the time off, until at the end of seven days it can be removed completely. I only mist sparingly if I see wilting during dome-off. Clones need warm temperatures to root. Seventy to 75 degrees Fahrenheit is about ideal, in my experience. Roots should be visible in seven to ten days. Seven to ten days after that, they're ready for big pots (or transplanting to outdoor plots).

CHAPTER 10

Gathering the Harvest

Step Ten: **Harvesting your crop can be the ultimate victory for any pot grower. However, the key to reaping the best marijuana lies in knowing when to harvest and how to cull your plants properly.**

Focus Points:
- **When to Harvest: Leaves, Flowering Male, Flowering Female Plants**
- **How to Harvest**
- **Stripping Plants Before Curing**

Short of actually smoking or eating the plants you grow, no part of the growing operation offers greater satisfaction than harvesting the fruits of your labors. It's a sweet feeling to take two or three hits from a spicy-tasting, potent bud that was nurtured by your own hands, and then realize that this stuff rates with some of the best you've smoked. Maybe it's just prejudice—gardeners always say that the tomatoes from their own crops are the sweetest—or maybe marijuana that has been hand-grown, harvested, and cured with personal care is better than stuff grown by the hectare and shipped by the bale from down south.

When to Harvest: Leaves, Flowering Male, Flowering Female Plants

The key to knowing when to harvest is to observe your plants and to look for signs of peak THC content.

All cannabis plants produce THC throughout their life cycle as an insect repellant. The chemical can be found in each part of a marijuana plant (stems, leaves, stalk) but the potency and amount of THC is negligible except in the leaves and buds of a plant. More importantly, THC will build up in each biological structure, but the cutoff

This is what you've been waiting for: thick, fragrant buds.

Although just 3 feet tall, the top spike of this *indica* yielded an ounce of bud.

for THC production will be different depending on which part of the plant you're working with. In other words, the amount of THC in a leaf will plateau once that leaf turns fully green and stops growing. However, an unfertilized female bud may continue to build up THC content for six to ten weeks after first flowering, depending on the strain.

Most seed sellers will offer instructions on when to harvest (again depending on which strain or strains you initially purchase). However, if you're working with a mix of strains or if you've culled seeds without instruction, then your approach will be more instinctive than scientific.

Leaves

You should have been pruning your plant along the way (see **Chapter 6**) so you may have an idea of how potent your leaves are by the time your marijuana starts to flower. If you've been pruning simply to focus on removing yellowing or dying leaves, then you may have been waiting for the right time to start culling leaves for smoking. Basically, THC content tends to plateau once a green leaf is fully extended. You can definitely gather some grass while your plant is still in the vegetative state. However, you want to make sure you've got a balance going between pulling leaves and allowing for growth. If your plant is strictly vegetative, then pulling too many leaves at once will stress the plant and may cause delayed flowering or trauma.

If your plant has moved into the flowering stage, you'll want to ignore the leaves closest to the buds. These leaves will continue to build up THC content along with the flower itself. So if you clip too early, you'll basically be ripping yourself off.

Flowering Male Plants

Generally male plants produce less THC overall than female plants. But seeing as you can still get a great high from males (plus I've never been one to advocate sexism)

Harvesting leaves as your plant grows will help induce flowering.

This top bud in early September will flesh out and become larger in the next few weeks.

harvesting males can be just as rewarding as harvesting females. The general rule of thumb is that THC content is highest for males right before they pollinate. So you're looking for fully flowered male plants with hanging pollen sacks that are visible but not yet open. (Remember to keep a few male plants intact if you want to pollinate for next year's seeds.)

Flowering Female Plants

Harvesting an unfertilized female plant is the ultimate reward for a marijuana grower. As with male plants, flowering will occur at different times depending on which strain you're working with. The characteristics you want to look for in a ripe female bud all depend on the color of the reproductive organs of the plant. A female marijuana plant has hairlike "pistils" that rise up from the flower. These will appear white at first, but as they approach peak THC content, the appendages will appear toasty gold or brown. In addition, the buds and top leaves of a flowering female plant will be covered in tiny stalks of THC-filled resin. This gives the plant a dew-covered or frosted appearance that comes from almost microscopic growths called "trichomes." Trichomes appear when a female plant is in full bloom, and each individual trichome tends to resemble a tube with a beach ball at the top. The THC content is highest at the "beach ball" top of each tube, so be careful when you finally do harvest. The trichomes will reach peak THC content when they are clear or milky white. If they appear to turn amber, the THC is starting to degrade as the trichomes collapse and start to decompose.

How to Harvest

If you're an indoor grower, the harvesting process is fairly simple: Uproot the plants to be harvested, then hang them upside down (more for convenience than any other reason) in the same grow room. If you're planning on creating a new crop, you can replant your pots now and keep your lights on for twenty hours a day, drying your harvest even as you sprout the next crop.

Outdoor growers typically just pull up their plants by the roots, knock the root balls free of dirt, and lash the females (males will already have been harvested several weeks prior) together just above the root balls, sometimes two or three plants per bundle. In

The white pistils on this plant indicate that the bloom is not yet ready to harvest. The plant can still produce more THC in this bud.

large commercial operations plants are typically just hung in a warm, dry place to cure over the next two or three weeks.

Stripping Plants before Curing

This is a wonderfully tedious segment of the personal-use farmer's growing experience. If you've been successful, anticipate spending many busy hours removing individual buds intact from their main stems with sharp, long-bladed scissors—bear in mind that your buds are reservoirs of next year's crop seeds, and treat them gently. Leaves can be removed and stashed for a rainy day, or left to dry until not quite crunchy, and then ground into a flour for cannabis oil or butter. Unlike commercial growers, you will probably want to trim off everything not worth smoking; a point to remember

if you decide to weigh your yield, because your harvested and cleaned pot will lack the four or five grams of nonsmokable stems found in an average ounce of street weed.

Growers are likely to find a lot more seeds in the buds they harvest than are found in any of the bags they've purchased from dealers—in fact, you shouldn't be surprised to learn that half of the weight of your buds is comprised of seeds. A pot dealer who sold buds with the volume of seeds produced by fully pollinated females would soon be ostracized (at the very least) by people who paid him premium prices for mostly seed.

For me personally, more seeds than I need is not a problem, because

Flowering females the first week of September.

the more seeds my plants produce, the more I will plant, even if it's just tossing handfuls of them into roadside ditches. I keep several hundred fat, perfect, hand-picked seeds in reserve for planting next year's personal crop, of course, but it seems fitting that the abundance of seeds that is provided by nature when plants are left to pollinate freely should be sown at least as freely.

Removing seeds from your own smoke can be a sticky, tedious, but still kind of fun after-harvest chore. Begin by snipping off each individual bud from their parent stem with sharp scissors and placing them into a bowl. Next, roll the removed buds lightly between your thumb and forefinger, feeling for seeds, then gently dislodging them to fall into a collection vessel. Many will be covered by a thin green membrane of plant tissue—which is itself covered with THC crystals.

A top bud with large shade leaves trimmed away in preparation for curing.

Top bud.

Lashing and hanging plants is the accepted method of harvesting for growers who handle hundreds, even thousands of plants per season. Personal-use growers who harvest perhaps thirty plants a season often use other methods that aren't cost-effective on a larger scale. One of my personal favorites is to wait until end-buds have matured enough to have fully developed seeds, then snip off only the fat ends, leaving smaller, lower buds to continue to grow for as long as possible while you prepare the proverbial cream of the crop for smoking.

Taking a mature top bud from a stalk or branch.

CHAPTER 11

Curing and Storing Your Crop

Step Eleven: **The best way to ensure year-round satisfaction is to make sure you've protected your crop. The techniques for storage are simple but vital for combating mold, mildew, and general spoilage.**

Focus Points:
- **Drying the Crop**
- **Storage for a Year**

If a grower's crop is anywhere near successful, the harvest will be too large to stash in a cupboard or dresser drawer, and you'll be stuck with the happy task of preparing at least a year's supply of smoke for long-term storage.

Besides the peace of mind that comes with knowing that the cannabis you're putting into your body hasn't been sprayed with insecticide or herbicide, the reason for growing personal-use marijuana is to ensure yourself of a good supply of the kind bud until next harvest. That means putting a year's worth of cannabis into storage, where seeds will not be damaged by freezing, buds will neither mold or grow stale (a number of experts claim that stored marijuana will actually increase in potency for the first several months—I can't say that I've ever noted an increase in the stoning, but aged weed does seem to be a smoother smoke).

A single female cannabis plant can produce more than an ounce of good bud.

A freshly picked bud (top) with a cured bud that's ready for smoking.

Learning how to prepare, dry, and store your crop is a skill set that just keeps on paying for itself. You'll be glad you took the time to learn now, when you relish your ability to pull weed out from storage year-round. It's equally important to remember that a year's worth of work can easily be ruined by slacking off at the end. Placing green marijuana into storage without preparation almost guarantees that it will begin to mildew, then become moldy.

It is not advisable to smoke marijuana that has gone moldy, because, depending on the species, you could give yourself a serious, even fatal, lung infection. Cooking with molded marijuana seems to be okay, so long as preparation involves temperatures of at least 350 degrees, but even then it is recommended that all foul-tasting mold be scraped off beforehand.

Drying the Crop

Drying is the most common method of preparing fresh marijuana plants for storage. But within that seemingly simple stage of the growing operation there exists a multitude of different methods and opinions about how it should be accomplished.

Hanging the Buds

Traditional methods of drying plants—the way it's done by large-volume commercial growers—is to simply pull up mature plants by their roots and then hang them upside down in a dry place until nearly all moisture has evaporated from their tissues. Plants are not hung upside down to allow THC to "run" from the roots into the foliage. In fact, the primary reason plants are hung upside down is for convenience; it's just

Crushed buds being air-dried.

easier to hang them in that orientation—the same reason that tobacco leaves are still hung by their roots for drying. A cord lashed around the stalk, below the last branch, is held securely in place when tied, unable to slide past the plant's large root ball.

Another important reason for hanging freshly pulled marijuana plants is to permit them to expire more slowly. This practice is conducted for the same reason that it is used to "cure" tobacco leaves whose smoke would be disagreeably harsh and unpleasant tasting if they were quick-dried artificially using heat. Being uprooted and dying sends a plant into high-gear survival mode, one result of which is a high level of simple plant sugars in the tissues, and a less-bitter chlorophyll. And like tobacco, those phenomena of the curing process have the effect of making the marijuana you process for smoking

Curing plants can be as simple as hanging them until they are dry enough to be chopped up and smoked, much like tobacco is dried, as shown here.

into a product that is palatable, pleasing to the nose, and as gentle on the lungs as it is hard-hitting to the brain. In fact, some growers maintain that proper curing is necessary for coaxing maximum THC levels from a harvested plant.

Ideally, plants hung to cure should be under a roof to block out harsh sunlight that might dry plants too quickly and unevenly. It's also important that falling rain be blocked from literally washing away THC from the outsides of curing bud, and of course to keep drying time to a minimum. Open air tobacco-curing sheds—essentially just a roof supported by posts—are probably best, but not always feasible; backwoods growers often accomplish the same purpose by stringing a green tarpaulin in the form of a peaked roof between trees, over a taut "clothesline" hung with drying plants.

Curing time is very dependent on humidity and ambient temperature, but figure on leaving plants—especially females with large, dense buds that have more moisture content—to hang for at least a week in dry 70-degree weather. Most growers concur that thoroughly desiccated marijuana foliage is not the best smoke; for maximum smoothness and minimum harshness, your bud or leaves need to contain a percentage of

Hanging plants to dry and cure need not be a complex operation.

moisture that allows them to burn less hotly with more smoke. Leaves that are at prime dryness will have turned dark green, but not yet brown, with slight dry crunching at the edges, but a tough and fibrous consistency throughout the leaf. Buds will feel dry and slightly crunchy on the outside, but sticky (the stickier the better) when squeezed between thumb and forefinger.

Air-drying the Leaves

Air-drying is the best method of drying leaves or whole harvested plants because it retains the most of a plant's pleasantly fragrant scent and spicy taste. In the case of midsummer leaves trimmed from plants during normal pruning, the best way to air dry them is to bag the loosely wadded foliage—"fluffed" to maximize the airspace between leaves—in an airy sack. Two unsophisticated favorites are a plain brown

Paper bags are very good for drying cannabis because they draw moisture from plant material and dissipate it to the outside.

Leaves and buds dry well in a covered cardboard box.

paper bag and a net-type fruit sack. A paper bag, its top folded over several times to seal it, steadily and evenly absorbs moisture from inside, then dissipates it to the outside; shaking the bag from time to time to redistribute its contents helps them to dry more rapidly. A mesh onion sack containing loosely crumpled leaves is a favorite among pot growers who dry small amounts for personal use, because the netting provides for maximum air circulation and the shortest drying time.

When drying marijuana for smoking using any of the methods covered here, it isn't necessary or desirable to dry it to the point of being crunchy. Foliage that is just moist enough to be flexible, but dry enough to burn evenly with a smooth, sweet smoke when chopped fine with scissors produces a superior smoke with leaves or bud. Air-drying is the only safe way to dry buds from which you intend to gather seeds for another crop.

A pile of smaller (i.e., not spikes) buds next to the pile of shade leaves removed from their stalks.

Microwave Leaves or Buds

If you need to make leaf or bud smoking-dry in a hurry, a microwave is ideal. More than that, it's a handy tool for growers who frequently need to dry small samples of their crops for test smoking. Samples of an eighth-ounce or so can be quickly dried by placing uncut foliage in a heavy coffee mug and microwaving it at high power for one minute. Larger portions can be placed, about an ounce at a time, into paper lunch sacks whose openings have been folded over to close them, and microwaved for a minute at a time. At the end of each minute, remove the bag and shake it to help dry its contents; if you have more than one bag to dry, rotate them, letting one or more cool and dry while another is being nuked. Again, the dried pot will smoke best if you leave it just slightly moist. Do not use a microwave to dry buds from which you intend to gather seeds for next year's crop, because the radiation kills the seeds.

Convection Oven for Leaves or Buds

Large amounts of marijuana can be quickly dried in the gas or electric convection oven of a kitchen range. Spread plant material thinly over the bottom of a large ungreased cake pan, then place it into an oven set no higher than 150° F (excessive heat appears to diminish potency). Turn drying plants every fifteen minutes, taking care not to overdry them. Be warned that this method will also likely kill all seeds in any buds you dry, so growers will want to clean their buds prior to baking.

Still slightly damp, this plant is ready for smoking.

Sweetening the leaves

Regardless which of the previous methods you elect to use for drying pruned leaves, their smoothness and taste, for smoking and for baking, can be maximized by "sweetening" them. Sweetening is a process by which fresh green foliage in a ziplock bag is first bruised by crushing it, then stored for no more than twenty-four hours (lest it should mold) in the sealed bag in a warm place. Just as bruises on fruit quickly become sweet as they overripen prematurely, allowing fresh pot leaves to die slowly causes them to increase the manufacture of sugars as they expire, and keeping them sealed in an airtight bag (or jar) for half a day or more makes even lowly leaves take on the taste and smell of fine bud. At the end of that curing period, remove foliage from the airtight bag and dry it for smoking or cooking.

Open Skillet for Leaves and Buds

This method of drying marijuana brings back memories of squatting next to a campfire in the deep woods, shaking an aluminum campfire skillet filled with fresh-picked marijuana over hot embers until the plants were dry enough to smoke. The same technique has worked well using an iron skillet over a propane camp stove in a remote cabin and in a household kitchen.

Fast-Curing Buds

If you're like me, you're going to want to sample the results of your labors as soon as the buds ripen—especially if this is your starter crop, and there aren't buds to smoke from last season's harvest. Over the years I've worked out a speed-curing method that enables small batches of buds to be dried quickly for immediate consumption, because it's just too intriguing to wonder how good this year's crop will be. Besides, having an ounce of good pot to smoke (or eat) takes the anxiety out of waiting for the rest of your crop to cure.

The trick is to retain as much of the buds' flavor and potency as possible, and the obvious tool for that job might seem to be a microwave oven. I don't recommend using a microwave to dry buds because ultrahigh-frequency radio waves kill seeds contained within them. Also, microwaves heat from the inside out, which is effective for drying buds, except that it also overheats them, detracting from their taste and possibly from their potency. If you must use a microwave to dry damp cannabis, be sure to remove all seeds first (they tend to explode anyway), break material to be dried into fine pieces, and never heat it for more than a minute at a time.

The method that works best for me so far is to snip off the buds I want to smoke, then place them in a ziplock bag that is sealed with all of the air squeezed out of it. Then I knead the buds from outside the bag, making them warm to "activate" THC contained in them (much the same as making finger hash). I may even stand on the bagful of buds in shoeless feet, squashing them with my heels until they become warm, wet with their own juices, and very dark green, almost black, in color (this operation does little or no damage to the seeds, which are protected by the diameter of the woody stalks to which they re attached). At this point I leave the bag sealed overnight, and may even sleep with it under my pillow to keep the contents warm.

After about twelve hours, I remove the warm, crushed buds from their plastic bag and lay them neatly—with air space between them—on a dry, clean cookie sheet. Preheat your kitchen oven to its lowest setting—usually somewhere between 150 and 180 degrees—and place the cookie sheet of crushed buds inside for half an hour. After that, remove the sheet and turn the buds over. Replace the cookie sheet for another half hour. At the end of that time, the buds should be just slightly moist, and a little sticky—ideal for smoking. Gently remove the seeds, which are usually not harmed by this mild heating process, place the seedless buds into a coffee mug, and with large scissors chop them into pieces small enough to smoke.

Storage for a Year

Black-market marijuana doesn't need to be entirely dry because it will be repackaged and sold quickly to users.

For sellers, moist pot weighs more, and most smokers prefer a modicum of water vapors to make their marijuana burn with a gentler smoke (I've seen unscrupulous dealers add a full ounce to vacuum-packed pounds by adding an ounce of water and letting it soak into the buds before repackaging them into ounce bags). But if you're

Commercially cured and packaged marijuana buds seized by the DEA.

putting up a crop of nice buds (and leaves) that must last you for the next twelve months, until next year's harvest, the same conditions don't apply.

Mold and mildew are the personal-use grower's biggest foes after harvest. I once watched, a little awed, as a veteran pot dealer dispensed with 25 pounds of very good bud in less than twelve hours; you, however, will face storing a pound of harvest (maybe more) for up to a year. Moisture in any concentration is a bad thing for marijuana unless it is vacuum-packed (which still only slows the formation of mold), so the annual stash should be thoroughly desiccated before storing. It can be rehydrated later for smoking by adding a few drops of water per ounce, and letting it sit in a ziplock bag in a warm room for several hours.

If the cannabis to be stored is too damp (you'll feel the moisture by squeezing buds between thumb and forefinger), you can dry leaves with no more than a minute at a time in a microwave; buds are best dried on a cookie sheet in a kitchen oven that's adjusted to its lowest heat setting. Don't microwave buds dry unless you first remove any seeds you might want to plant later.

The ideal environment for storing dried marijuana is much the same as for any dried or packaged vegetation: Store in a cool, dry place. Attics are perfect, so long as they are free of mice and squirrels that may actually eat your stash unless you store it in glass jars. Garages and barns are also good, but you must remove seeds intended for planting before winter can freeze them in northern latitudes, and it's a good idea to package it in rodent-proof containers.

Alternately, harvested marijuana can be frozen like any vegetable for more than a year without fear of mold or loss of freshness. This is probably the best way to store your harvest, but only in places where laws have been relaxed sufficiently to let you get

Storing cured buds in airtight bottles—preferably with a moisture-absorbing silica packet—keeps them fresh for months.

away with it. If you freeze, be sure to remove the seeds for next year's crop before you do, because freezing a seed kills it (that's why cannabis doesn't reproduce by itself in places where the ground freezes in winter).

Packaging

The icon of black-market marijuana is a flap-top sandwich bag filled with buds taken from 1-pound "bricks" that have been vacuum-sealed in heavy-gauge plastic bags. The bricks themselves may have entered the end-user marketplace immersed in engine oil or other liquids at the bottom of an open-head barrel, in the sewage tank of a motor home, or in the vermin-infested bilgewater of a seagoing vessel. In so many cases in recent years, young smokers have come to associate the smell of pot with the faintly similar but sickly sweet fragrance of dryer sheets—placed in many shipments

The most common way of packaging marijuana is to place it in plastic bags, sometimes vacuum-sealed to remove all air that might assist in the growth of mold.

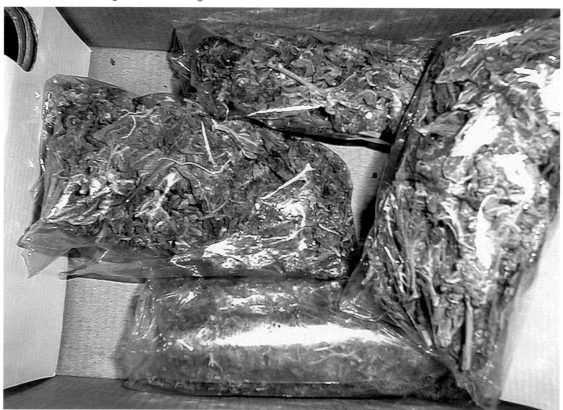

of smuggled cannabis to confuse the noses of drug-sniffing dogs. All of these are good arguments for growing your own cannabis and for packaging it with personal care and more security. The packaging of commercial pot headed for market isn't selected because it is necessarily the best method of containment, but rather because it suits the purposes of the people transporting and selling it. Again, handling a hundred pounds of bud meant for sale on the streets is less personal than preparing your own stash, and personal-use growers can do themselves and their harvest better service than just stashing it in baggies.

Storage Containers

In places where marijuana is still an illegal plant, growers need to be aware that packaging their harvests into the usual 1-ounce plastic bags is often constituted by courts as evidence of felony dug trafficking; the legal reasoning being that only a drug dealer would have possession of more than one small, salable package of marijuana.

The fact is that it's impractical, and even harmful to your harvest, to store it all in a single container, where a little mold on one damp bud that escaped you can quickly spread to all of the weed in that container. For that reason alone, it's a good idea to segregate a supply into smaller units that are isolated from the others. And if you're especially prudent (always a good trait in today's world), you might want to divide your stash into several scattered caches that ensure you won't be wiped out if someone stumbles onto one of them.

Look around the house for small containers you can recycle for storage purposes.

My preferred method of caching dried and ready-for-storage marijuana is to first package dry, uncleaned (filled with seeds) buds and cured leaves separately into 1-quart ziplock backs. The bags are filled only a quarter-full of cannabis, then a moisture-absorbing silica-gel packet—scavenged from electronics packaging, foodstuffs, and other products that normally include them—is inserted. Then I roll the pot rolled up inside the bag, bottom to top, squeezing out as much air as possible, and I seal the zipper lock. A pair of rubber bands, one at either end of the bag, help it to maintain a mold-fighting vacuum, while keeping it in a convenient cylindrical shape.

With my smoking weed packaged into rolls that contain less than 1 ounce of marijuana—because possession of an ounce or more is still a felony where I live, for now—I

Commercial marijuana packaged in tube form.

slide each bag into a mayonnaise or similar-size jar tall enough to accommodate them. Generally speaking, a jar that's tall enough to easily fit a rolled-up quart-size bag under its cover has a large enough diameter to hold roughly 1 pound of marijuana. Sealed inside a snugly capped jar—with another silica-gel packet or two thrown in for good measure—your bud is safe from the elements for at least a year.

Maybe I'm paranoid, but even that isn't good enough for me, and I like to double-protect my stored harvest by placing sealed jars filled with bagged marijuana into paint cans or plastic buckets with water-tight snap-down covers. These can then be buried or otherwise hidden in places where they aren't likely to be found by people—remember, legalized or not, your bud will always be a stealable commodity, so protect it, spread it around in several caches, and hide each one of them well. One suburban stash for folks who grow—or buy—their smoke in volume, but don't want to risk having a large amount of it in the house, is to loosen a square of sod in one corner of the backyard, bury a sealed plastic bucket of weed in the soil down to its lid, and replace the sod. For me, it's paint cans inside hollow stumps back in the woods; even a military ammunition box with lock-down waterproof lid wrapped in a garbage bag and buried in a shallow hole camouflaged with ground debris. Whenever I run low, or need extra smoke for the holidays, I know where I can get another ounce or more with a quick trip on snowshoes.

PART FOUR

Enjoying the Fruits of Your Labor—

SMOKING EQUIPMENT, MAKING HASHISH, AND COOKING WITH POT

CHAPTER 12

Smoking Equipment

Here is a rundown of the basic, and not so basic, tools needed for smoking your crop.

Smoking recreational drugs, from jimson-weed and opium to peyote and crack cocaine, just to get stoned has been done since before biblical times. Smoking is the fastest and most common method of getting one's brain under the influence in minimum time because drugs suspended in smoke are quickly absorbed through lung linings and directly into the bloodstream. Problem is, smoking requires equipment.

Focus Points:
- **How to Roll a Joint**
- **Toke Stone**
- **Arrow Tokers**
- **Basic Pipes**
- **Bongs**
- **Vaporizers**

I recall being at a deer camp where a friend and I weren't scheduled to be picked up from the remote swamp we were hunting for fourteen days, and having an ounce of really great bud, but no pipe and no papers. Such is the driving motivation for a true pothead

Bongs, pipes, and stones all provide easy smoking experiences.

to get baked that my friend arose early the first morning and shot a small buck for us to eat during our stay. Then he cut 6 inches off the knuckle end of a leg bone with the saw on his multitool, and used his survival knife to drill a one-inch bowl in the flat behind the slightly flared joint. The marrow was hardened by boiling and removed from the bone's core in pieces with a length of fence (and snare) wire whose end had been bent into a hook. Then a length of fence wire was heated red in the fire and used to poke small holes that opened bowl to stem. It was crude—some even called our bone pipe "gross"—but it kept a pair of stoners far from civilization tuned in for two weeks. That bone pipe served well for the next four years, until age and heat made the bone brittle and it broke while being cleaned one day.

Rolling a joint is the classic method of smoking marijuana, but many people find a pipe or bong easier to master.

How to Roll a Joint

Isn't it amazing how many people who smoke pot claim to be incapable of rolling marijuana in a cigarette paper into a clean-smoking joint? Enough; it's time for all you nonrollers to learn to twist a joint. I smoked roll-your-own cigarettes for twenty years—not tapered-end movie cigarettes, but squared-end smokes that were often mistaken for Camels or Lucky Strikes—and I can't abide a joint that doesn't smoke well.

The infamous blunt is a cigar that has been slit lengthwise, emptied of tobacco, refilled with marijuana, and usually stuck back together using the roller's saliva.

Rolling a good joint begins with having marijuana that is the proper "grain" to both roll well and burn evenly. Consistency should not be powdery, as this is both difficult to keep inside a paper and will tend to smolder and "run," burning unevenly on one side but not the other. Makings that are too coarse can also make a joint run, and may result in a bumpy, homely looking doobie that no one can take pride in. The ideal pot for rolling a joint is somewhat coarse, about the consistency of fine mulch, and slightly moist—moist marijuana not only rolls more easily but also has smoother smoke.

There are enough types, sizes, colors, and even flavors of rolling papers on the market to confuse someone who isn't high. It is my assertion that none is better than another if the objective is to get stoned by smoking a joint. Beginners usually find a larger paper easier to work with, and one edge should be gummed, to help keep the joint stuck together. Beyond that, it really doesn't matter which paper you choose.

Grip the paper at the corners of its ungummed edge between the thumb and forefinger of either hand. Then, slide your middle fingers upward along the underside of the paper, forming it into a trough. Hold the paper in that shape with one hand while the other sprinkles a thimbleful of marijuana into the trough.

With the paper held in a trough shape between thumbs and middle fingers of both hands, smooth the marijuana being rolled with your index fingers, pushing just a bit more to the ends than is in the paper's center (this helps to ensure that ends remain tightly rolled as the joint is smoked). Next, place your index fingers atop and alongside your middle fingers, and use your thumbs to gently roll the marijuana at either end back and forth to form it into a tight cylinder. When the ends feel firm and evenly cylindrical, roll the ungummed edge upward and tuck it under the other side of the rough, forming a tube of paper filled with marijuana. Smooth the joint's outer surfaces by gently applying thumb pressure as you roll the tube back and forth toward the gummed edge. When you have the joint at dimensions you can live with, roll the ends tightly toward the gummed edge, give the glue a lick, and stick it down to hold your tautly rolled, even-burning joint in shape

Joint Smokers

The problem with a joint is that it leaves a butt. "Roach" butts are not only smokable but also represent the most potent portion of a joint. Having had all of the inhaled smoke passed through it, the butt end becomes saturated with THC-laden resins and oils. If the objective is to get THC into your bloodstream, then smoking a joint to ash is an effective and efficient use of marijuana.

Toke Stone

I suppose we'll never know who created the first toke stone, but it was a product of the latter twentieth century, when power tools became inexpensive enough for everyone to own them. Sort of a pipe for smoking joints, a toke stone is nothing more complex than a soft stone—clay, lime, or soapstone, usually—that has had a hole drilled through it from one end to the other, creating a wind tunnel of sorts. A tapered-end joint is inserted into the hole at one end of the stone, then lighted and toked on from the hole at the opposite end of the stone.

Making a toke stone isn't a challenge. First, select a soft stone; most preferred are thick disc-shaped stones, like the water-smoothed stones found at shorelines. This shape enables a lighted joint in the stone to be set onto a table or counter surface while keeping the burning ember suspended in midair, where it won't burn anything. And if

There are millions of places to buy beautifully designed smoking equipment like the bong pictured. But if you get a little creative, you can also make your own bong that is just as effective and far cheaper than the fancy supplies.

you want your stone to look like an authentic Cheech and Chong prop, the flat surfaces also make good, if small, canvases on which to express one's inner self in paint.

Next, fix the stone in a vise in a position that best accommodates the direction you mean to drill from—the drilling process is much easier if you have a drill press to keep stone and drill immobilized, but it has often been done using a hand drill. Determine where you want to drill, pop on your safety glasses, and start drilling using a new, sharp masonry bit in a plug-in power drill. Diameter of the drill bit determines how large or small a joint can be smoked through the stone, but ⅛ inch should be appropriate for all but the stingiest friends. The bit should start burrowing into the rock with little downward force, leaving behind a residue of fine powdered stone. It helps to keep the hole flushed and lubricated with plain water as the bit bores more deeply. When the hole is bored clear through, smooth away nicks and sharp edges around the openings with coarse (fifty-grit) sandpaper. Insert a joint in one hole, light it, and smoke from the opposite end until it's gone.

Arrow Tokers

This supersimple joint smoker consists of nothing more than a 6-inch (or whatever length you prefer) section of aluminum arrow tubing—broken arrows are fairly common at archery ranges, where they'll often give them to you for asking. A ⅛ inch-diameter hole drilled through just one side, about 1 inch from whichever end you choose, is about the right size to accommodate most tapered-end joints. With one end of a fat hooter stuck into the hole, place one index finger over that end of the arrow

A simple water bong made from a maraschino cherry jar, two brass rifle cartridges, and a length of latex tubing.

tube to block it, and draw a hit from the opposite end. Keep your index finger over the other end as you toke, forcing all air drawn in to pass through the lighted joint, then, just before you can't inhale any more smoke, remove your finger and let a rush of fresh air drive the smoke you've inhaled deeper into your lungs. Arrow tokers are lightweight, concealable, and not likely to be recognized as smoking paraphernalia. They also let you smoke a joint down to virtually nothing without burning your lips.

Another version of the arrow toker is a head-rush tool known as a "steamroller." This simple joint smoker is made the same way as the arrow toker, except that it uses an aluminum tube an inch or more in diameter in place of arrow shaft. The larger tube is still smoked with its end blocked off by your palm as you inhale through the opposite end, but when you release it at the end of a long hit, and the smoke filling the tube is allowed to rush into your lungs, the effect is one worth experiencing.

A fifteen-minute pot pipe made from an oak dowel and a brass firearm cartridge.

Basic Pipes

The most basic tool for smoking any type of material that a person wants to inhale is an old-fashioned pipe. With a pipe, a smoker draws outside air through a bowl filled with burning marijuana, accelerating its burn rate and increasing the heat of its ember. Smoke is pulled from the bottom of the bowl through a drawing tube that terminates at the smoker's lips.

Slightly more inventive pipes (and bongs) add a "carburetor" hole that is kept plugged by a finger or thumb tip while a smoker is drawing on a lighted bowl. When

A marijuana pipe made from a piece of pine and a sawed-off brass .308 caliber rifle cartridge.

the burning bowl glows red and the stem or expansion chamber is filled with billowed smoke, the carburetor hole is unplugged to let air flow fast and freely to the smoker's lungs. Similar to the ram-induction hood scoop on a muscle car, the sudden rush of wind drives smoke deeper into the lungs, resulting in a more of it being absorbed.

In the creative hands of marijuana smokers, the pipe has evolved into a variety of specialized tools that bear little resemblance to the briars and corncob tobacco pipes smoked by pre-hippie beatniks of the early 1960s. Purpose-built pot pipes of today range from beautiful multicolored blown-glass to ornate worked-brass models, and even works of art carved from soapstone.

Bongs

Have you ever seen one of those crazy-expensive Rainbow vacuum cleaners? You don't have to be an engineer to deduce that the guy who designed this machine knew the mechanics of a marijuana bong. The Rainbow's fame stemmed from a system that brought in dirt from the outside to be exhausted into a tank half-filled with water. Dirt, dust, and other particulates were exhausted at the bottom of the water tank, where they were trapped by being made wet and too heavy to pass into the impeller motor's exhaust to the outside.

That is essentially the concept behind a water pipe, except that this venerable old design uses a smoker's lungs to provide the suction force necessary to efficiently consume a vessel of burning marijuana—sometimes opium and other drugs, and sometimes in a "hookah" unit with several hoses for group smoking. In every form, a bong is a sealed suction unit, with outside air concentrated and drawn by vacuum through a lighted bowl, which accelerates the combustion of its contents. Smoke from this enhanced combustion is pulled to the bottom of a small water tank, where it is exhausted into water, which cools it and traps ash and other particulates. Smoke that fills the airspace above the water is smoother to inhale and easier on the lungs than if it would be without the water barrier between bowl and mouthpiece.

The bong I remember best from my childhood was a monstrous contraption with three rubber hoses that we called the "pickle jar bong," because the body of its construction had once held kosher dill spears. Using only a knife and the sometimes frantic advice received from friends who were anxious for some means to smoke their weed, I had drilled a hole through the center of the jar's screw-on lid, just large enough to accept a copper fuel-line tube

A blown-glass bong.

Pot-smoking paraphernalia can be made from any number of household items.

if I twisted and wiggled it through. With the cover on the jar, the copper tube sat on its bottom and stuck up from the top one inch. An expended .308 Winchester rifle cartridge with its base cut off and a small piece of metal window screen pushed into the cut end served as a convenient bowl; its narrow neck fit neatly into the copper tube, after a little shaving with my knife. Around the jar lid's perimeter, I carefully drilled three slightly smaller holes with the tip of my knife, then forced three 8-inch hoses of latex surgical tubing (we used it for our wrist rocket slingshots) through those holes from the top. The soft hoses sealed themselves, but I sealed the jar lid to the copper tube—making their joining airtight—with a generous layer of fifteen-minute epoxy. Even before the epoxy had begun to set, we had the jar half-filled with water and the filled bowl glowing red. That was actually good, because our combined suction, which probably approximated that of a small Shop-Vac, drew the rapidly hardening resin into any leaks, sealing them right away. That pickle-jar bong burned pounds of marijuana over five years before someone who must have really needed a bong stole it.

PVC-Pipe Bong

This bong hearkens back to the hippie culture of the '70s. There are many variations (pot smokers are a creative lot), but the basic unit consists of a PVC pipe—or any tube—about 2 inches in diameter by 10 inches to more than 6 feet long. The bottom end of the tube is sealed with a flat glue-on PVC cap that allows the tube to stand on end. A hole drilled about 4 inches above the capped bottom should be just large enough to accept whatever metal tube you might opt to slide through that hole. Ideally, the tube—typically copper fuel or hot-water line—has an inside diameter of 1/4 inch, just the right size for a respectable joint. The metal tube angles through the drilled hole from the bottom of the capped tube to about 3 inches beyond its outer wall. Seal the hole around the metal tube with a generous application of quick-drying epoxy, and let it harden. Finally, a pencil-size carburetor hole drilled about 4 inches above and slightly to one side of the metal tube give the bong a lung-filling kick that is limited only by the length of the PVC tube used.

Probably most people are familiar with this bong configuration, because it seems to be an icon of pot smokers in the movies, and it works the same way. Fill the bottom of the tube with 3 inches of water (I've also used sweet wine or sometimes bourbon). Insert a lighted joint into the open end of the metal tube, place an index finger over the carburetor hole, place your mouth in the PVC tube's opening, and suck. When your lungs feel about half-full, release the carburetor hole and let the tubeful of smoke flow into your lungs. This bong can also be used dry, and the tube end can be flared using a tube flaring tool and turned into a bowl. Push a faucet aerator or section of steel window screen down into bottom of the conical bowl to hold burning pot in place, and have yourself a party.

Soda Can Bong

This is a northern redneck emergency bong that has gotten many a carload of good ol' boys stoned when someone had weed, no one had papers, but everyone had a metal can containing some sort of beverage. By indenting the bottom end with a cross point screwdriver or some other tool that will make a conical depression in the metal, then punching a pin-size hole at the bottom of the cone, an impromptu bowl is formed; it can be oriented with the can's drinking hole in any position that suits you. Finally, punch a small airhole through the can's bottom to serve as a "carburetor."

Fill the conical bowl of your can bong with some shredded bud, seal the drinking hole with your lips, and block the carburetor hole with the index finger of the hand holding the can while you apply a butane lighter to the pot. Inhale as much as you can, and just before you hit your limit, release the carburetor and let the canful of smoke rush into your lungs.

Vaporizers

Vaporization is the latest way for modern humans to smoke pot. The machines use direct or indirect heat, usually generated by power supplied from a household outlet, to completely incinerate herb placed in their combustion chambers. According to stoning experts at *High Times* magazine, vaporization is an efficient method of smoking marijuana, it's healthier than smoking joints or from pipes, and is "gaining thousands of converts each month."

A big part of the vaporizer's appeal is that it can stretch your pot supply about twice as far for most people. With some of today's ultrapotent bud selling for $400 an ounce, a catalytic combustion system that delivers twice the high from a bowl of weed, with much less irritation to the respiratory tract, has tremendous appeal to apartment smokers. Vaporizers effect more efficient extraction of THC from the bud they burn, incinerating tars and other particulate by-products that irritate bronchial passages. For regular smokers, a vaporizer might pay for itself in a few months.

As might be expected of an industry in which CEOs stay stoned as part of the job, there are a lot of vaporizers on the market at this time, in many price ranges and configurations. Basic units begin at around $60, ranging to more than $500 for a portable outdoor party unit powered by rechargeable lithium-ion batteries. While that diversity enables consumers to select from a larger array of models to find one that best suits their needs and pocketbook, it can also result in a lot of confusion. Probably most

The Amazing BC VAPORIZER!

"Your Healthy Alternative"

Vaporizers use an electrically heated element to convert marijuana into relatively clean, cool smoke that is easier on the lungs.

cannabis vaporizers are purchased online, sight unseen except for a thumbnail and a more-or-less-complete list of specifications. Following are a few tips that every smoker shopping for a vaporizer should keep in mind.

Vaporizer Heating Systems

At this time there are two methods by which vaporizers apply intense heat to marijuana in their combustion chambers: Conduction and convection. With conduction, or "hot-plate," models, the cannabis to be smoked is placed on a hot plate that is heated by a nichrome (toaster) wire that glows red-hot when electricity passes through it. Contact between the herb and the heated element completely vaporizes the marijuana. Not as efficient as most convection models, conduction vaporizers are usually less expensive and more portable than convection models, and are far more efficient than the carry-around, portable (and usually inefficient) glass and metal types that need to be used over a kitchen range or other type of open-flame burner.

Convection models are better, in terms of efficiency and smoking smoothness, but these are generally more expensive. Instead of applying marijuana directly to a red-hot element, a convection system drives a stream of superheated air (currently 360 to 430° F) through the pot being smoked. Similar in principle to the flameless process that transforms wood into charcoal for summer barbecues, the flow of superhot air reduces marijuana to carbon without actually burning it. The process produces cool smoke that is more gentle than bong smoke, while at the same time being comprised of finer particulates that are more readily absorbed by a smoker's lungs—like what a turbo-charger does by converting gasoline to an aerosol before it's burned. The clean heat of convection causes resinous glands, or trichomes (psychoactive cannabinoids that are the source of kif) in the outer layers of cannabis to literally "evaporate." The cloud of smoke released by this process is said to be cleaner than with conduction models, with better stoning and less coughing.

CHAPTER 13

Hashish

Now that you're proficient in marijuana growing, you may want to familiarize yourself with other products you can produce from your crop.

Hash (short for hashish) might be most accurately described as concentrate of cannabis. It is made by separating THC-bearing sap (resin) and "crystals" from coarser plant fibers, so that you are left with the essence of marijuana. This condensed product is several times denser and more powerful than the marijuana would be if it were simply cured and smoked. Hash at its most basic is a pastelike substance that varies in pliability. As a small grower you may not want to take the time and effort to make your own hashish. Nevertheless it's a topic that's bound to come up at some point. The topics below are not instructional so much as it is informational. Knowing the basics of hashish will help you decide if it's something you may one day want to pursue as you progress as a grower.

Focus Points:
- Laced Hash
- Moroccan Hash
- Nederhash
- Hash Buds
- Kif
- Resins

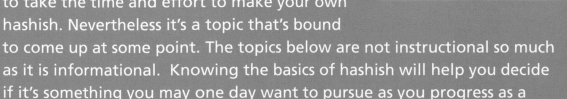

Laced Hash

"Commercial" black hash often contains opium—something to be aware of before you find yourself waking up in a strange place. A flood of opium from Afghanistan in recent years (I can't help but see images of Air America in Vietnam) has found its way into hash sold on the street, sometimes in ratios as high as 50 percent. The addition of raw opium into the poorest-quality hash turns it into a potent smoke, sometimes too potent for casual pot smokers who aren't prepared for the often nauseating and sometimes paralyzing effects of opium smoke. Opium-laced hash can usually be identified as having a pliable and sticky texture; it will have a sickly sweet smell before burning that will become stronger when it is burned. Like opium, the smoke of opium-laced hashish seems to continue expanding in your lungs even after you've stopped inhaling. If you suspect the hash you're smoking is doctored with opium, I recommend taking no more than three hits before waiting at least fifteen minutes to see how powerful its effect will be.

Howard Marks, one of the most successful hashish smugglers in English and Canadian history, once described how tribesmen on the border of Pakistan and Afghanistan made a form of hashish known as border hash. The technique he saw them using entailed pounding cannabis plants—leaves, buds, green stems, everything but the woody main stalk—with a seesaw assembly that suspended a large pounding stone from one end of a long pole placed over a fulcrum of logs. By applying leverage, a single person at the opposite end of the pole could raise a stone weighing several hundred pounds and lower it like a primitive press onto green plants placed in a giant clay or carved-stone bowl that was heated over a low fire. The stone crushed and mixed the heating plant tissue, supposedly crushing the resin sacs and "activating" the THC with heat. (This runs contrary to the common belief that applying heat to green marijuana destroys its THC content.) When the heated plant mass had become a black, tarlike mass, it was allowed to cool and harden before being cut into pieces.

The Rif Mountains
of Morocco

Another, potentially more dangerous, additive that is sometimes found in both black-market hashish and marijuana is crystal meth. This cheap bootleg methamphetamine is not impressive when I recall Christmas parties of the 1970s that had candy bowls filled with multicolored Benzedrine and Dexedrine pills that were more effective and less damaging to their users. I've smoked ganja laced with meth, and the effect on me and the people I smoked it with was unpleasant, with increased heart rate, elevated blood pressure, and profuse perspiration along with a short-lived speed buzz. Those effects could be lethal to an unsuspecting smoker who suffers from hypertension, any cardiac troubles, or diabetes. I'm not sure what effect the addition of crystal meth has on seeds within a bud, but growers who sow them should probably not get their hopes up.

A very simple black hash, called "charas," or "finger hash" is made by kneading soft plant tissues with the fingers (thus heating it) until it is rendered into a tarry mass. Spread the mass out onto a flat surface until it is thoroughly dried and hardened (three or four days, depending on ambient temperature and humidity), and break it into stoning-size chunks before wrapping it in aluminum foil.

Shaman pipe for smoking hashish

Moroccan Hash

Probably the best-tasting hash is the least processed. One favorite is a primo-quality recipe from the Rif Mountains of Morocco in which resin is extracted by using a stout club to pound whole green plants against a dished-in rock. The congealed green resin that forms on the rock's surface is scraped away with a knife, then gently pressed in half-inch layers between two sheets of fabric, where it is left to dry and harden, then broken into chunks for smoking. This type of unheated hashish is generally agreed to be the sweetest smoke, but its potency of course depends on how powerful the plants it was made from. It falls into a sack and is then gently pressed. It doesn't get touched by hand and is not heated. It has the purest sweetest flavor (when it's top quality).

Nederhash

In Holland, where decriminalizing pot has spawned a very lucrative industry of hash and marijuana cafés, pot professionals make a truly ass-kicking hashish called "Nederhash" from superstrong Dutch hydroponic weed. The color quality of Neder-hash varies from blond to almost white. Light brown or green varieties are that color because of an excess of plant material in the collected resins (intentionally added by unscrupulous manufacturers to increase weight), usually with a general reduction in potency. Nederhash is typically made in small quantities, so recipes, taste, and quality vary, but if any client of an Amsterdam hash café has ever been disappointed, I haven't heard of it. The Dutch use a small, commercially available machine that resembles a hobbyist's rock tumbler, called a "Pollinator," to gently tumble marijuana stems, buds—the whole plant—thus knocking loose THC crystals and resins. When a powder of crystals has accumulated in the bottom of the tumbling jar, they are poured onto a clean ceramic dinner plate or metal pie tin, and gently pressed into a soft mass. The attraction of Nederhash is that it is usually very fresh because it's made in small batches. Unlike

A note of warning: Even in places where anti-marijuana laws have relaxed to the point of effectively decriminalizing possession and use of cannabis, both hashish and kif are nearly always regarded as manufactured drugs, in the same category as methamphetamines and heroin. The penalties for just possessing either is the same as it would be for those potentially harmful drugs, so keep that in mind should you decide to try your hand at making either.

"imported" black-market hashish, which can be stored for years in a sealed canning jar, Nederhash has a tendency to mold, and it should be smoked immediately or kept frozen.

Hash Buds

When the buds I've grown finally reach maturity, I want to sample some of them right away—again, part of the fun of planting seeds from a bag of "street" weed is that you might end up with a number of different strains with sometimes very different buds. When I don't want to wait for buds to cure by air-drying, I speed-cure them by placing trimmed buds still on their main branches into a heavy ziplock freezer bag, then squeezing and kneading them from outside the back until they change from green foliage to a damp, almost black mass. As with the finger hash described earlier, the warmth of being kneaded activates THC within the buds and brings out the resins; in short, this actually increases the potency of buds, and even enhances taste and smoothness by increasing the release of sugars from cellulose. Hash buds must be smoked right away, because they are damp, dense, and prone to mold. Exposing the massed buds to the open air or to very low heat—about 150 degrees—on a clean cookie sheet in an oven dries them, but you can smoke from damp black buds within a couple of hours of their removal from a plant. Just

tear a small bud from the main stalk, place it over a pie tin, and gently massage the bud between thumb and forefinger to roll hard, round seeds that have grown from the main stem free of the smokable bud that surrounds them. Seeds are sheathed within a protective green membrane that is as smokable as the bud. (White or light green seeds are immature and not likely to sprout; the darker and fattest seeds are the best choices for storage for next year's crop.) Using scissors or just your fingers, shred the remaining bud into a loose, airy mass that will dry quickly in open air. If you're really in a hurry, you can give the shredded bud thirty seconds in a microwave, after which it should be dry enough to smoke—remember, slightly moist weed has a sweeter, less acrid smoke than completely dry leaves or buds.

Kif

Literally, Kif—sometimes spelled keef or kief, and usually pronounced "keef"—translates from the Arabic as "what," while the term "kif-kif" means "the same as" (I leave the reasons for their association with the recreational drug by that name to the reader). Kif is a traditional marijuana derivative that continues to be a favored recreational drug in Morocco and the Middle East. There are several definitions of the word kif, including a mixture of tobacco and marijuana bud or hashish laced with kif powder that is traditional in Morocco.

Kif also describes a collection of unadulterated THC-laden "crystals" that are removed from the outside of mature cannabis plants by gently rubbing their parts against a fine-mesh metal screen or cheesecloth. The powder that falls away drops through the cloth or screen and is collected onto a plate. Then, like hash resins that are beaten or otherwise coaxed from inside plant tissues, the accumulated kif powder is lightly pressed into sticky sheets and smoked alone (a practice that seems generally unpopular among Middle Easterners), sprinkled as powder onto cannabis bud, or, most common, mixed with tobacco. Marijuana smokers in the United States have long reported employing a similar practice in which a tobacco cigarette is smoked after smoking a joint or bowl to enhance their buzz; an Americanized version of Moroccan tobacco kif can be seen in the "blunt," a pot-filled cigar that I used to really enjoy before I gave up tobacco.

Commercially manufactured kif boxes with fine grating screens held elevated an inch or so above their bottoms make it easy to rub free THC-bearing granules that fall

through the screen and into the box's bottom; if you don't have a kif box, a fine metal window screen or a section of coarse linen stretched over a bowl and held in place by rubber bands can suffice—I personally like the abrasiveness and easy cleaning of a screen made from no-see-um insect netting. With either type of kif collector, the harvesting process is as simple as lightly rubbing the outside of the marijuana being collected from over the abrasive screen, loosening THC-bearing crystals that fall through and collect in the bottom of the reservoir below. Some kif-makers prefer to extract powder from buds only (buds are still very much smokable after this operation); another school of thought maintains that buds should retain all of their potency, and kif should be collected from branches and stems that are too harsh to smoke by themselves. Kif can be collected from green stems (and leaves), but in my experience the job is easiest, with the greatest yield, after the parts being harvested have dried completely enough to snap when bent. An added problem—and also a benefit—encountered when collecting kif from green or damp plants is a buildup of hashish resin on the screen; this is most easily by allowing the screen to dry thoroughly for one or two days, then wringing the resins into a bowl if your screen is fabric, or gently scraping them free if your screen is metal.

Resins

If you smoke marijuana through a pipe or bong, tarlike resins left as residue accumulate each time you smoke, until the pipe's airways become clogged with sticky black globs that impede the flow of smoke and must be cleaned out. My favorite tools for this job with most pipes include a large pair of scissors and a long-shaft, small-blade flathead screwdriver—these pretty much cover my cleaning needs.

When you scrape out a copious glob of black goo with that first swipe down a clogged pipe's airway, you might be repulsed at first, but I like to repress the urge to scrape it into the garbage. Instead, I scrape the tar onto a book-size square of aluminum

foil, which I then fold carefully around it. Each time I clean my pipe or bong thereafter, I'll add whatever tars I collect from them to the mass inside the foil.

As weeks pass, the collected resins will dry and harden, until they resemble black hash—which they are, in a sense. At any time they may be smoked in a pipe bowl, but resin by itself burns poorly, requiring constant flame while toking, and it needs to be stirred frequently as fire encases the resin's outer surface with a hard shell of ash. The taste is generally not pleasant, tasting of already-burned pot, and the effects of smoking resin don't appear to be better than the buzz gotten from the weed it was formed from, despite having the illusion of being concentrated cannabis.

Some smokers mix cannabis tar with opium resin or other drugs to enhance its potency, but I prefer to blend warmth-softened resins into cured marijuana leaves that have been chopped finely or powdered in an electric coffee grinder. Mixed about fifty-fifty, the resulting "green hash" is smoother to smoke than pure resin, and the more easily combustible leaves help to make it burn cleaner and more steadily. Too, the body buzz of leaves in concert with whatever stoning traits might have been in the marijuana that created the tar can sometimes team up to create a very good high.

CHAPTER 14

Eating Marijuana

Cooking with marijuana is one of the best ways to enjoy your crop year-round. Below are several tried-and-true recipes that taste great and show you how to preserve the THC throughout the cooking process.

Focus Points:
- **General Notes on Preparing Marijuana**
- **Cannabutter**
- **Cannabis Brownies (from scratch)**
- **Cannabis Brownies (from mix)**
- **Sesame Skillet Cookies**
- **Happy Flapjacks**
- **Stoner Fudge**
- **Hemp Tea**

While *Cannabis sativa* is native across the globe in one species or another, not every culture—or individual, for that matter—prefers smoking as the delivery vehicle for getting desired components of the herb into your body. For some people, the best way to get the effects that marijuana can provide is to ingest it and let the digestive system absorb it as it passes through the intestinal tract.

A buzz induced by eating marijuana is slower coming on, taking thirty minutes to an hour to become noticeable, but the effect lasts longer, sometimes all day. A downside is that it takes about three times as much marijuana taken orally to achieve the same, quick effect obtained by smoking a joint. Advantages of eating pot instead of smoking it include not hurting your respiratory tract and soothing an upset stomach, making it possible for chemotherapy and other patients whose treatments induce nausea to eat without vomiting.

General Notes on Preparing Marijuana

Obtaining maximum potency from the pot you cook with depends on how well it is absorbed into the bloodstreams and brains of those who eat it. Plant cellulose, often lumped under the blanket term "fiber" by dieticians, is hard to digest—that's why it works to scrub out a person's colon. It follows, then, that a plant as rough as cannabis will be hard to digest, and the less it is broken down and absorbed, the lower the percentage of THC that will be absorbed from it.

Low heat releases THC from within a plant's fibers, making it more accessible to our bodies, but maximum potency can be achieved by making plants more digestible. For me, the simplest solution is one that had been used by American Indian tribes for thousands of years, but was only verified by modern science in 1996: A teaspoonful of wood ashes added per gallon of whatever mixture is to be cooked works to break down complex proteins, converting them to usable amino acids that are more easily metabolized. Wood ashes by themselves have a salty, slightly biting taste because of their mildly caustic nature, but become tasteless when cooked into a recipe.

This dried cannabis leaf has been ground to flour using an inexpensive electric coffee grinder.

Cannabutter

Cannabis butter is a delicacy of gourmet weed smokers who like to have the option of eating their way to a usually gentle, long-lasting buzz. Sautéeing marijuana in butter is said by some to enhance THC absorbed from the marijuana, although it seems more likely that the heat applied activates THC crystals in the plant's outer trichomes—much the same as it does when preparing black hash. Whether that's true or not, cannabis butter is a great ingredient for making cooking cookies or, especially, brownies whose dry ingredients already include powdered marijuana.

Begin with a small saucepan over your stove's lowest burner setting—better to take too long than to ruin your work by burning it past edibility. Add one quart of water and bring it to a rolling boil.

Melt two sticks of butter (220 grams) into the boiling water, stirring constantly. When the butter has melted and is blended well, add a quarter-ounce (about 7 grams) of finely chopped, cleaned, and seedless marijuana; leaves are fine, as are finely chopped leaf stems, but buds make the most potent product, of course. Some weed gourmets prefer to make cannabutter with green, fresh-picked marijuana, because the juices in its tissues transfer more readily into the butter.

Stir the marijuana into the gently boiling butter-and-water mixture, then cover and let simmer on low heat for forty-five minutes, stirring frequently. After forty-five minutes, remove the pot from heat and let cool for six hours, stirring every thirty minutes.

After six hours, reheat the mixture to liquid consistency and separate the marijuana by pouring it through a wire strainer held over a bowl. Refrigerate the bowl for one hour—until the butter has hardened across the top of the bowl—and pour off the liquid again; what remains is cannabis butter.

Cannabis butter may be spread onto toast, pastries, or hotcakes, or it can be used to satisfy the requirement for butter in recipes. You can also use the leftover marijuana from this operation as an ingredient in other recipes.

Cannabis Brownies (from scratch)

Ingredients

8 1-ounce squares of unsweetened chocolate

1 cup cannabutter

5 eggs

3 cups sugar

1 tablespoon vanilla

1 ½ cups flour

1 teaspoon salt

1 cup chopped pecans or walnuts (optional)

Instructions:

Preheat oven to 375 degrees F. Grease a 9 x 13 pan. Then mix dry ingredients first to ensure that they are blended thoroughly. Beat eggs, sugar, and vanilla at high speed until smoothly blended. Melt chocolate and butter in a saucepan over low heat. Blend in molten chocolate, flour, and salt. Mix well until just mixed.

Pour batter into lightly greased (nonstick spray is fine) prepared pan, and bake for thirty-five minutes or until a toothpick inserted into the brownie comes out clean, with no wet batter on it. Cool and frost, if desired.

Cannabis Brownies (from mix)

Ingredients:

1 box of brownie mix

½ cup vegetable oil (or whatever is required by box instructions)

2 eggs (or whatever amount of eggs required on your box)

1 ounce of dried cannabis leaves, finely ground in a coffee grinder

1 cup chopped walnuts (optional)

Instructions:

With a large skillet preheated over low heat, pour the oil required by the brownie mix into the pan. Heat the oil on low heat, for five minutes, then mix in powdered marijuana. Stir constantly for five minutes, until the mixture emits a pleasant, almost nutty, aroma, then remove the pan from heat and allow it to cool. Be careful to not let the mixture overheat, or the oil may become unpalatable; do not allow oil to get hot enough to smoke, and remove the skillet from heat immediately if it does begin to smoke.

At this stage there is an argument among pot-brownie bakers over whether the cannabis-oil mixture should be strained to remove larger particulates from the oil. "Strainers" maintain that heating in oil extracts all of the pot's THC, rendering the plant matter into "nothing more than grass," to quote one expert. Nonstrainers argue that sautéed marijuana is still marijuana and helps to enhance the effects of brownies in which it is included. I'm of the opinion that if the marijuana has been powdered in a coffee grinder, it can be left in the oil; it's tough to strain it out anyway, it will digest better because it is already so finely broken up, and except for a pleasant spicy taste you won't even notice its presence.

When the cannabis oil has cooled, stir all ingredients together in a mixing bowl until the contents take on a thick but smooth and creamy texture. Add nuts, raisins, or dried cranberries if desired.

Pour the mixture into a greased 9-inch cake pan (larger if you want thinner brownies), and bake in a preheated oven at 325 degrees for about thirty minutes, or until a toothpick inserted into the pan's center comes out dry.

Sesame Skillet Cookies

Ingredients:

- ¼ teaspoon nutmeg
- ¼ cup honey
- ½ teaspoon ground ginger
- ¼ teaspoon cinnamon
- ¼ ounce seedless, stemless, finely chopped cannabis
- ¼ cup toasted sesame seeds

Instructions:

Mix all ingredients in a bowl until well blended. Set aside.

Place skillet over low flame and grease with 1 tablespoon of salted butter. Add batter, cover skillet and cook over low heat for five minutes, or until center is dry.

Remove cooked cake mixture from the skillet and allow to cool. When cool, cut the cake into strips and roll them in sesame seeds.

Happy Flapjacks

Ingredients:

1 cup powdered marijuana, leaves or buds

1 cup Jiffy or Bisquick baking mix

1 ¼ cups whole or skim milk

1 egg

4 tablespoons cooking oil

Instructions:

Gently sautée marijuana and oil in a small skillet over low heat to "activate" the THC, adding more oil if the mixture is too dry. Stir constantly until a pleasant nutlike smell emanates from the mix, but be careful not to burn it.

Add the sautéed marijuana and oil to the other ingredients and blend the mixture until smooth and creamy. The proper consistency should run from a ladle slowly but steadily, like a very thick paint. Place one ladleful in the center of a large preheated and greased skillet over medium heat. When holes begin to appear at the outer edges, gently loosen them around their perimeter with a spatula. When holes begin to form near the flapjack's center, slide the spatula under the pancake's center and flip it. After thirty seconds on that side, the flapjack is ready to eat.

Stoner Fudge

Ingredients:

4 cups granulated sugar

1 cup cannabutter

1 7-ounce jar marshmallow creme

A candy thermometer

2 5-ounce cans evaporated milk

1 12-ounce package semisweet chocolate chips

1 teaspoon vanilla extract

A 10x12-inch cake pan

Instructions:

Combine sugar, milk, and cannabutter in a large (1 gallon) covered cooking pot. Cook at medium heat, stirring constantly, until the mixture begins to boil. Keep stirring constantly—it's critical that you don't burn it—for about ten minutes, or until the temperature on the thermometer reaches 236° F (about 20 degrees hotter than boiling).

Remove the boiling pot from the heat. Stir in chocolate chips, vanilla, and marshmallow creme. (It helps to microwave the opened jar of marshmallow creme for about twenty seconds to soften it and make it come out of the jar easier—watch it, though, because the sticky stuff can quickly overflow.) Stir until thoroughly blended, and pour into the greased cake pan. Makes about forty 2-inch squares, each of which should get an average person high.

Mixing semisweet baking chocolate with two tablespoons of cannabutter per pound of chocolate makes a nice after-hours treat.

Hemp Tea

Ingredients:

1 stainless-steel tea ball with screw-on cap and hanging chain
⅛ ounce of finely chopped (not powdered) stems and leaves, green or cured.

Instructions:

Fill the tea ball with chopped cannabis and screw its cap into place. Green cannabis has a "fresher" taste than cured pot, because of the chlorophyll in its tissues. Do not pack the cannabis into the tea ball, but allow enough looseness for water to circulate completely through the chopped pieces.

Place the filled tea ball into a mug filled with boiling water, and let the marijuana steep into the water for at least fifteen minutes, dunking the tea ball up and down occasionally to flush juices from the plant material into the water. Remove the tea ball and reheat the mug in a microwave. Flavor the tea with lemon, creamer, sugar, or just drink it plain.

Cannabis Grower's Resource Guide

On the presumption that every one today is either online or knows someone who is, the following short list of website links has been compiled to help direct growers to seed and growing equipment retailers who have virtually everything a beginner or expert needs to grow a successful crop of sweet and potent buds. Be aware that there is a lot of coming and going where cannabis-related websites are concerned, and any of these links might go offline any time. But they will always be replaced by new cannabis entrepreneurs, and probably most of what a grower needs can be purchased locally.

420 Hemp Shop: http://www.420hempshop.com

Amsterdam Marijuana Seeds: http://www.amsterdammarijuanaseeds.com

Marijuana Growing Supplies: http://www.search420.com

Medical Marihuana, Canada: http://www.medicalmarihuana.ca

Pollinator Company: http://www.cannabisseeds.com

Pot Smokers Net: http://www.potsmokersnet.com

Pot TV Network: http://www.pot.tv

We Be Stoned: http://www.webestoned.com

Weeds That Please: http://weedsthatplease.com